ENGLAND

An Illustrated History

ENGLAND

An Illustrated History

HENRY WEISSER

HIPPOCRENE BOOKS, INC.
New York

ISBN 0-7818-0751-4

For information, address:
HIPPOCRENE BOOKS, INC.
171 Madison Avenue
New York, NY 10016

Cataloging-in-Publication Data available from the Library of Congress

Printed in the United States of America.

CONTENTS

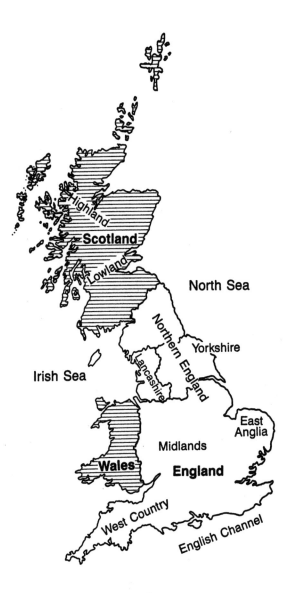

Early English History

(smaller scale than following timelines)

Tudor England

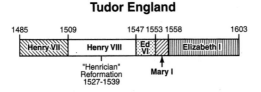

The Stuart and Hanoverian Eras

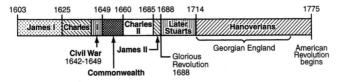

The French Revolutionary and Victorian Eras

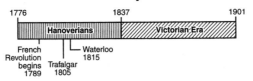

The Twentieth Century

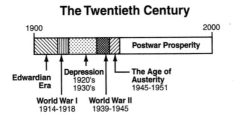

THE IMPORTANCE OF
ENGLISH HISTORY

English history is rich, complex, and of immense importance to many parts of the globe, including the United States. This crowded, small island has long been populated by dynamic and creative people who have left an enduring legacy. In this illustrated history I hope to clarify English history by sorting out its main strands and describing the truly important events, personalities and developments in a concise, comprehensive manner.

The term "British" applies to the English, Welsh and Scottish together. Wales was linked to England in the 16TH century and to Scotland in the 18TH century. In this book exclusively Welsh and Scottish history is deliberately omitted, but in recent centuries English history has become British history to a large extent. Therefore English history and British history have been treated synonymously in the later sections of this study.

Visitors in England cannot avoid exposure to historical references such as "the Stuart era," "Jacobean," "since Lloyd George was prime minister," "Norman keep," "Anglo-Saxon foundation," "Wars of the Roses," or many other designations from the past. History is truly a living and highly appreciated heritage in England—constantly reinforced by an enormous physical legacy in the form of cathedrals, castles, stately houses, inns, walls, parks, old villages, graves, statues, paintings and memorials. History is also present in customs, institutions, names, costumes, entertainment and countless other reminders. It is simply impossible to avoid history in England because it is everywhere, and at the very heart and essence of the English experience.

English history is especially important for Americans. After all, British history is American history before 1607, the year when Jamestown became the first permanent English-speaking settlement in America. From Jamestown until 1776, the year of American independence, a span of 169 years, American history was intertwined as a branch of British history. During this time, language, customs, laws, institutions and beliefs which had been derived from hundreds of years of experience in England were rooted in colonies along the Atlantic coast. Afterwards, essential components of English civilization continued in the young American Republic.

An example of this transfer from English history is seen in that quintessential American environment, the frontier, a place so often credited with shaping American character and destiny. Even the most American of figures in this American environment, the sheriff, evolved first in the forests of Anglo-Saxon England as the *Shire-Reeve*. The posse of the American "Wild West" actually began as the "posse hundredi" of England in the early Middle Ages.

Since American history was actually derived from English history, such figures as Henry VIII and Elizabeth I belong to all Americans just as much as they belong to all Britons. Indeed, many Americans know quite a bit about these monarchs while they know little about the colorful French rulers on the throne during the same century. Furthermore, events in English history such as Magna Carta and the Glorious Revolution of 1689 had much to do with how Americans have come to view the power and obligations of government. The very familiar, powerful American notion of free people enjoying certain rights and liberties first developed in England. So did the means to curtail the arbitrary power of governments.

2

Other nations have profited immensely from English history as well. Canada, New Zealand, and Australia are among many nations that had direct influence as parts of the British Empire. Many other far-reaching nations have come to emulate practices, laws and institutions that evolved in England, including due process, trial by jury, and a parliamentary form of representative government.

The greatest achievements in English history have been political. Over the centuries the English have shaped successful institutions and laws which have worked. They also developed political skill, enabling them to proceed gradually and to compromise when necessary. The overall result is a generally benevolent history, certainly more so than that of France, Germany or Russia. In England, economic and social progress and improvement have lasted for centuries while institutions have proven flexible enough to evolve with a changing society. The last time English government was altered by violence was in 1688. No other major European state can look back upon such a long, unbroken continuity.

Security through sea power allowed English history to proceed without outside interference. Except for sporadic incursions of troublesome Scots, England has not been invaded since 1066. For five hundred years the English have won all of their wars, except for the American Revolution, which the English prefer to interpret as a kind of civil war. Excluding this contest, Britain gained territory in each of its many wars. British explorers added even more, and by the 19TH century Britain had the largest empire the world had ever seen, thus guaranteeing the global significance of British history for years to come.

ENGLISH HISTORICAL GEOGRAPHY

Geography is a key to understanding the history of a nation. The most striking feature of British geography is its insularity, the condition of being an island. The term "Britain" refers to the island where England predominates in the east and south. Wales is to the west and Scotland is to the north. Much of English history has been determined and conditioned by the salt water moat surrounding it, which is just over 20 miles wide at it narrowest point in the English Channel. Whenever major developments occurred in Europe, such as the Reformation or the French Revolution, the English manifestation was always different because of insularity. The United States also shares this phenomenon: an ocean east and west which conditions American responses to European events.

Britain is by no means a large island. No location in Britain is more than 70 miles from the sea. Britain in its entirety is only 94,525 square miles, meaning that it fits into the state of Colorado (104,100 square miles) with 10,000 square miles to spare. (Perhaps Oregon, of similar size, 91,132 square miles, would be more appropriate for the purposes of comparison, considering its cool and rainy coastal region.)

Britain is a gentle, green country which has always provided an agreeable habitat for humans, animals and plants. The soil in the south and east is rich. The north and west tend to be hilly areas with poorer soils. Nature in Britain does not overwhelm. There are no impassible deserts or mountain ranges, nor are there torrential rivers or formidable swamps. The rain-fed rivers of Britain gently flow towards the sea; the mountains are old and worn, and the highest peaks only reach a few thousand feet. Marshy areas, called "fens," were common before

4

becoming drained in recent centuries. England's chilly, wet weather is constant, and extreme weather such as blizzards, heat waves and tornadoes do not occur. There are some rough, wet wastelands called "moors," as well as open, sandy seaside hills called "downs."

The effect of the Atlantic on Britain's climate is paramount. The ocean cools the island in summer and warms it in winter. Were it not for the warm flow of the Gulf Stream bringing up water from the south, Britain might have a climate similar to Labrador, which actually occupies the same latitude as the British Isles. Prevailing winds from the west lift clouds of moisture out of the Atlantic to drench Britain yearlong, thus guaranteeing a wet and chilly climate in all seasons that is ideal for plants, if not always comfortable for people.

England is the largest and richest part of the island of Britain, comprising 56 percent of it, mostly in the form of a gently undulating plain stretching away to the south and east of the rough, hilly country of Wales and Scotland. England itself can be divided into several regions. (See map page vii.)

East Anglia is a remarkably flat area bulging out on the eastern part of the island. It is similar in topography to the Netherlands, which is directly across the North Sea. The "Midlands" are undulating plains, and the "West Country" juts out into the Atlantic along the southern tail of Britain. The latter is noted for its rough topography and excellent harbors. The "south" is a term sometimes used to describe counties south of the Thames, a rich and gentle region closest to Europe and well-populated since ancient times. The "north," an area north of the Midlands, contrasts sharply with the "south." It is rougher and colder and, in recent centuries, its subsoil resources have been heavily exploited by industry.

Two important historic counties in the north are worth noting: Lancashire and Yorkshire. The former is associated with the very first developments of the Industrial Revolution. Old, historic Yorkshire, before its recent division, was so large that it was declared the "Texas of England." The map shows the old, historic counties, excluding the new subdivisions. North Yorkshire has stark moorland, as well as ruggedly beautiful stretches of green hillsides and valleys called the Yorkshire Dales.

England's gentle, wet climate, rich soils and thick forests lured many groups of invaders in ancient times. Wave after wave arrived, usually from the plain of Europe closest to Britain. In recent centuries no invader has been successful. At first this seems odd, considering that ancient invaders had primitive craft and the most recent would-be invader, Hitler's Germany, possessed the internal combustion engine. Yet the explanation of this paradox is that an island is easy to assail if its inhabitants are divided, while a unified island controlling the surrounding seas is very difficult to invade. The Spanish, French and Germans all learned this lesson in a very costly manner.

The economic advantage of England's proximity to Europe and athwart the sea lanes of the Atlantic has been well appreciated in recent centuries; but, in ancient times, the Mediterranean Sea was the center of civilization. Back then, Britain was seen as a chilly, remote and forested island on the fringes of Europe occupied by savages.

PREHISTORIC ENGLAND

The longest phase of human existence was prehistoric. In England this period lasted somewhat longer than it did in the

Middle East or the Mediterranean because, according to a traditional definition, history does not begin until there are written records. The Romans were the first to provide them for Britain, beginning around a half century before the Christian era began. By this definition of history, all that came before was prehistoric.

What we know about prehistoric Britain still remains obscure. Despite archaeological research and recent discoveries, what actually happened is subject to theory. Folklore abounds about this period, celebrating such people as the Druids, who were mysterious priests, and the great female warriors who went to battle in chariots.

What we do know is that wave after wave of invaders came ashore and subdued parts of the island. Warfare for territory seems to have gone on incessantly. Weapons evolved from stone to bronze, to a mixture of copper and tin, and then to iron. Archaeologists have given the groups of invaders various names based upon traces of evidence about them. Research indicates that, for a time, they were parasitic upon nature, hunting and gathering their food. Later, they became symbiotic with nature, raising certain plants and keeping certain animals domestically.

"England before the English" is one description given to the era because the English were the Anglo-Saxons and they did not arrive until 400-600 A.D. The earlier inhabitants are commonly known as "Britons" or "ancient Britons."

The most famous and powerful Britons belonged to a widespread group called the Celts. They came to Britain fairly late in the prehistoric period and were divided into many tribes. Iron-using Celts invaded around 400 B.C. The degree to which they absorbed the earlier inhabitants or destroyed them is unknown. Moreover, just who the Celts were, how they lived, where they flourished in Europe and where they originated from

7

remain keenly-debated historical mysteries. Scholars argue whether the Celts should assume a linguistic, cultural or ethnic classification. What we do know is that they lived on farms and villages, and that kin groups were important. Their art could be dazzling in its beauty and power.

Today only one independent nation of Celtic background exists: the Republic of Ireland. Scotland, Wales, the West Country and the French province of Brittany are other parts of the world with a marked Celtic heritage. In England itself the Celtic Britons were first conquered by the Romans and then overwhelmed by the Anglo-Saxons.

There are several impressive monuments in Britain left by what were very small prehistoric populations living close to subsistence. Many enduring prehistoric structures are in the form of megaliths, or specially arranged large stones. Stonehenge is the most famous of these sites, standing bold and magnificent on the plains near Salisbury. It is assumed that the huge stones, 30 feet high, were dragged from a quarry 20 miles away. A recent computerized study has strengthened earlier speculation that Stonehenge was built for the purpose of sun worship. If this is true, it is yet another indication of the immense, compelling power of religion within human society.

ROMAN BRITAIN

It is difficult to conceive of a period when Britain was a remote frontier rather than a vital center of civilization. Yet this was precisely the case during the long period when the far-flung Roman Empire included Britain. The Romans ruled this wet and cold frontier region far from their sunny Mediterranean

Stonehenge.

center for approximately 400 years, *c.* 43 B.C.– 450 A.D. (To go four hundred years back from the turn of this millennium in 2000 would put an individual in the last years of Elizabeth Tudor!)

The Romans left testimony to their skills in engineering all over Britain. Stretching 73 miles across the narrow neck of northern England from sea to sea, eight to ten feet thick with a fortress every mile, is Hadrian's Wall, a massive defensive barrier designed to keep the fierce northern peoples out of Roman Britain. Many sections still remain today in impressive form. Many Roman villas, temples, baths, floors and statuaries have been excavated by archaeologists. In other locations Roman structures were incorporated right into medieval walls, gates and roads—tributes to how the Romans built things to endure.

Prehistoric times ended for Britain when Julius Caesar fought a few brief campaigns in Britain from 55 to 54 B.C. The reasons for his arrival have been debated. Surely the Celts in Britain were allied to his Celtic enemies on the Continent; and, by invading Britain, he hoped to weaken his foes and protect his flank from an attack from Celts based on the island. The lure of slaves, possible gold discoveries and another triumph in Rome were undoubtedly additional incentives for his foray. Caesar's operations were brief, and the few Celtic tribes he subdued only paid tribute to Rome for a short while.

Conquest began in earnest a century later in 43 A.D., under the Emperor Claudius. His empire was peaceful, and thus its military forces were eager to find opportunities to ply their profession. At first, resistance was slight and southern England quickly became a Roman province. But, in 61 A.D. a fierce Celtic rebellion broke out under Boudicca, a tribal queen. She gathered and led a huge host of Celts who burned Roman cities

10

Hadrian's Wall across the north of England as it appears today.

Queen Boudicca, a modern, romantic statue which stands in front of Parliament today.

and slaughtered Roman citizens. Roman legions ultimately subdued the rebels, and Boudicca is said to have poisoned herself. The rebellion destroyed much and gained nothing. A romanticized statue of this queen, depicted as a ferocious woman in a chariot, stands near the Houses of Parliament today.

The most striking feature about the Roman period of British history is that Britain's historic role was reversed. Britain was then poor, weak and backward, subject to a distant imperial center boasting a higher civilization that could be measured by superior standards of living, cities, law, technology, literacy and culture. A thin layer of Roman officials, traders and administrators worked in provincial Britain. The Roman language, Latin, became the most important language on the island, and many Britons copied Roman ways to enhance their careers. The remaining conquered Celts worked for the Romans and paid taxes. Therefore, in many ways, Roman rule in Britain was very much like the hundreds of years of British rule in India.

Romanization was tied to urbanization. Towns were the strongholds of Roman civilization, where all the amenities of the ancient Empire were available. The countryside largely remained as it was in the Celtic era except for the great Roman villas which utilized slave servants—somewhat similar to the great houses of Southern plantations before the American Civil War.

The fall of Roman Britain, like the fall of the whole Empire, was not sudden. Sporadic raids from fierce Germanic people who had flooded into Europe, attacks from the fierce Picts in the north, and attacks from Celts in Ireland all contributed to the collapse of the Roman defenders. Rome itself was hardpressed on many fronts; in order to defend the core of their empire they had to withdraw their army legions from Britain and ask the inhabitants to defend themselves henceforth. Many

Romanized Britons were disheartened to see the legions sail away, knowing that they were now open to the furor of barbarian conquest.

Two Romanized Britons are famous. Both lived at the end of the Roman period during the barbarian onslaughts. One of them, St. Patrick, is famous for Christianizing Ireland. The other, King Arthur, has gone down in history as a Christian king who supposedly lived when knighthood was in flower. The romantic stories of his adventures with the Knights of the Round Table have been famous for centuries. In all probability, however, Arthur was a Celtic British native who adopted and upheld Roman Christian civilization against the invading floods of Anglo-Saxon pagans.

Despite the length of time that the Romans occupied Britain, the impact of their civilization on Britain was largely negligible. The Anglo-Saxons flooded into Roman Britain in such numbers and with such barbaric force from the fifth century onwards that they largely obliterated Roman civilization on the island. Besides, the invading barbarians despised urban life, which was the very essence of Romanization in Britain. Barbarians destroyed Roman cities and abandoned the ruins. The substantial physical remains from the Romans in Britain, mostly ruins and excavated sites, are more significant for understanding Roman history than for understanding British history because no spiritual inheritance from Rome came directly from their long occupation.

Although the Roman Empire became a Christian empire during the time it ruled Britain, the impact of the pagan Anglo-Saxons was so massive that Christianity was obliterated except for a few areas where it could survive, most notably in Wales. While the English language has a vital Latin component, this

13

did not come from the 400 years of the Roman Empire; it came indirectly from the Norman French following the year 1066.

THE ANGLO-SAXON INVASIONS

Roman civilization was extinguished during the bleak and violent "sub-Roman" period which extended into the European-wide Dark Ages, an era of barbarian conquest and settlement. England's experience during the Dark Ages was different from Continental areas. In other parts of the former Roman Empire, barbarians sought to seize the mantle of the Romans and continue the civilization they had conquered, no matter how cruelly. Therefore Continental barbarian rulers converted to Christianity and learned Latin, although their peoples soon corrupted it into the various romance languages. This pattern was not followed in England. There, the Romans and Romanized Britons had been few in number, and Romanization was quite superficial except for some urban areas. As a result, the massive tide of Germanic invaders swamped Roman civilization so thoroughly that neither Christianity nor Latin survived. Britain had to be re-converted to Christianity a century later. Those Latin components now in the English language came not from Roman Britain but from the Norman Conquest of 1066.

England's Dark Ages have been called the "blank page" of English history. Extending from the middle of the 400s to the beginning of the 600s, it is the most difficult and obscure period of English history, yet it provides the foundation for all English history thereafter.

These centuries remain obscure because they lack evidence of all kinds: The early illiterate Anglo-Saxons did not leave coins or inscriptions, and all of their wooden buildings were decayed. Written evidence for the events of this time period comes from chronicles prepared by churchmen hundreds of years afterwards.

We know that the Anglo-Saxons swarmed out of the river systems of northwestern Europe. They were a part of a vast migration of Germanic people who were being pressed from behind by even fiercer people moving through eastern Europe. Some were Angles, some were Saxons and some were Jutes, but they were all mixed together. The hyphenated name, Anglo- Saxons, is usually employed as a useful term to distinguish them from the Saxons who remained in Germany.

The Anglo-Saxons were a pagan tribal people, stereotypically tall and blonde. They extolled the joys of battle and hunting, and all of the virtues of endurance and bravery that these activities encouraged. Their invasions were undoubtedly fierce and bloody and, unlike the Romans, they did not want to occupy the Celts. Instead, they succeeded in driving most of them out. Celts fled to the rougher, less fertile country in the west and north. To this day Celtic people predominate in Wales and Scotland. Physical anthropology confirms the effects of this ancient ethnic struggle: Despite the easy mobility of modern populations, shorter, darker-haired people continue to predominate in Wales, and taller, blonder people continue to predominate in England.

It is a pity that historians know so little about the period of the Anglo-Saxon invasions because this was the time when England truly became English. The designations "England" and "English" are derived from words to describe the Angles, a name that was used for all Germanic invaders of Britain. These people became England's main ethnic stock as they flooded across the plains of Britain.

Over time the language of the invaders evolved into English, a fact revealed when comparing everyday words in English with everyday words in German. For example, "fuss" in German is "foot" in English; "tür" in German is "door" in English and so on. Many of the ways that the language is structured was also determined by the Anglo-Saxons.

The invaders brought tribal customs and laws that eventually evolved into English common law. They also far exceeded the Celts in mastering the environment. The Anglo-Saxons quickly became vigorous farmers whose iron tools were employed to clear the dense oak forests and plow the heavy clay fields of the midlands. Once they had settled firmly across the plains, missionaries from the Continent began to arrive to bring England back into the orbit of Christian civilization.

ANGLO-SAXON ENGLAND

Anglo-Saxon England occupies over six hundred years of English history. During this span, fierce tribal pagans became civilized Christians who were able to pass on a profound institutional, legal, spiritual and mental inheritance to subsequent centuries. The era came to an end when the Anglo-Saxons were conquered by the Normans; but these conquerors nevertheless utilized and preserved most of the elements of Anglo-Saxon civilization at hand.

The primitive law of Anglo-Saxon England involved the community with oaths and oath-helpers, ordeals, prices upon persons' heads, and legal obligations of kin groups. The fundamental aim of the law was to diminish violence by providing a sort of rough justice through fines and payments for wrongdoing. Here were the dim and distant origins of both the English and the American common law.

Patriotic English writers have celebrated the rights of Anglo-Saxon freemen, which included participation in community meetings and the right to bear arms. Some have traced the origin of Parliament and the jury system back to the forests of Anglo-Saxon England, but the evidence for such claims is fragmentary. In actuality, Anglo-Saxon society was stratified with an upper class of nobles called "thanes" (or "thegns") at the top and slaves at the bottom. Slaves comprised prisoners of war, convicted criminals, and children sold into slavery by their parents.

England was divided into several Anglo-Saxon kingdoms. The power and effectiveness of Anglo-Saxon kings had to be limited by the frontier nature of their kingdoms. Kingdoms were divided into shires, and a king's agent, called the Shire-Reeve, looked out for the king's interests in each of these subdivisions. This agent became the "sheriff" of British and American history. Sheriffs tried to enforce "the King's Peace," which at first protected certain persons, certain places and certain days. Over the centuries this royal peace expanded to more times and more places so that now the Queen's Peace exists all over England. That is why today's lawbreakers are cited for "breaking the Queen's Peace."

Anglo-Saxon England was overwhelmingly rural, with most people living on farms or in small villages surrounded by fields. The few towns, if large enough, were incorporated as boroughs. Burgesses were townsmen owning houses and shops. It may be noted that the first American legislature, which began to function in 1619, was the Virginia House of Burgesses.

Christianity returned from two different directions. Celtic missionaries came from the north and St. Augustine came from the south, sent by Rome. Canterbury in the southeast became the center of St. Augustine's operations after his arrival in 597. The two strands of Christianity sought alignment over matters of doctrine, organization, the use of Latin, calendar and dress. Interest in art and education was fostered by the church. While the Anglo-Saxons built many churches, very few still survive. The reason for this is that the Normans and their descendants usually built over Anglo-Saxon edifices.

The evolution of several Anglo-Saxon kingdoms was interrupted by ferocious Viking invasions. In some ways, the Vikings did to the Anglo-Saxons what they themselves had done to the Romans. They were a flood of pagan pillagers from overcrowded Scandinavia. Yet there were differences: The Viking conquest was only partial, and the language and many customs of the Vikings were similar to those of the Anglo-Saxons.

A Christian hero, Alfred, King of Wessex, resisted these Scandinavians heroically. Eventually the Vikings and their descendants were Christianized and absorbed into the population. They were particularly numerous in northeastern England, where they controlled an area called Danelaw for a time.

Some have compared King Alfred to Charlemagne because both fostered law, order, Christianity and learning during barbaric times. Many romantic stories center about this kindly, shrewd king, such as tales about what happened to him when he showed up here and there in disguise. Instead of slaughtering defeated Viking pagans, Alfred sought to baptize them. Many hardened Viking veterans are said to have endured baptisms.

The American connection to Anglo-Saxon England is substantial because our language, law, important elements of our

One of the few remaining Anglo-Saxon churches.

institutions and a substantial proportion of our ethnic stock are derived from it. Their world was a world of the forest frontier, so when a new frontier beckoned in North America, Anglo-Saxon folkways, customs and laws proved to be immensely adaptable and successful.

THE NORMAN CONQUEST

European-style feudalism was first imposed upon England by the Normans, who carried out a swift, bloody and brutal conquest of the Anglo-Saxons, beginning in 1066. This was the last invasion in English history. The Normans kept much of the society and institutions of Anglo-Saxon England intact, but they imposed themselves as an alien elite throughout the country. Everywhere, defeated Anglo-Saxon nobles were replaced by French-speaking conquerors. The language still bears evidence of their impact. Words of French origin still predominate for topics of diplomacy, war, politics, cooking, hunting and sophisticated human interactions. The richness of English is in part due to the fact that it frequently has two words for one thing, one from German and the other from Latin via Norman French.

By any measure, 1066 was a landmark year in English history—the year when William I of Normandy, known as William the Bastard, defeated the last Anglo-Saxon king, Harold, at the Battle of Hastings. William's invasion was a great gamble, and it almost failed not far from the coast as the Norman horsemen struggled to break the Anglo-Saxon wall of shields that blocked their advance. Cleverly feigned retreats by the Normans drew the Anglo-Saxons from their strong defensive position, and the death of Harold from a high-flying arrow turned the tide. The famous Bayeux tapestry records this desperate struggle in the woods of southeastern England where a mere eight thousand men changed the whole history of the island.

William was a cold-blooded usurper but, like all other conquerors, he fabricated a number of complicated claims to the throne of England. If the script for 1066 could have been written in Hollywood, William would have been the defeated villain, and the self-governing Anglo-Saxons and their heroic, democratically chosen and handsome King Harold would have saved the nation from conquest. In reality, the Norman Conquest was part of the violent world of feudalism. The surviving Anglo-Saxon lords found that they were stripped of their lands and titles and were permanently replaced by alien lords who were better at fighting and utterly brutal and ruthless when it came to imposing their control over the countryside. All of the Norman knights who were brave enough to sail with William were richly rewarded with confiscated Anglo-Saxon estates.

Who were these Normans who so rapidly imposed French feudalism and church organization on England? They came from Normandy, a seacoast province of France, but they were non-French in origin. These seething, restless conquerors were Frenchified Scandinavians, originally called Northmen, who had come south from what is now the region of Norway to conquer Normandy. This was accomplished just over one hundred years before their invasion of England was launched. They rapidly learned French methods of administration and how to fight effectively as armored horsemen.

Once in authority, the Normans energetically transformed the superstructure of England. They left their hallmarks in massive stone constructions. Many cathedrals, churches and castles today boast of their Norman portions or foundations. Massive

A medieval depiction of Norman soldiers aboard a ship.

A church arch shows the massiveness of Norman construction. The lamp is modern.

Norman arches and columns are unmistakable and testify to the sheer power of the conquerors.

The Normans were the very last conquerors of England, and they did the job completely and ruthlessly. The richly detailed Domesday Book is a testament to their thoroughness. It was literally a richly detailed census of all that they had taken, useful for administration. Its name comes from the feeling that its judgments were as permanent as those that would come to the world on the day of its doom.

Like many successful conquering elites in history, the Normans allowed the conquered to keep as much of their old culture as was compatible with their rule. For a time there was an ethnic dichotomy in England, as Normans imposed themselves over the Anglo-Saxons. The rulers had a different language and culture and were never overthrown. Instead, they were absorbed over a few centuries by a two-way cultural and biological diffusion. The Normans and their culture simply amalgamated with England's Anglo-Saxon base because of intermarriage and the fact that there were relatively few Norman families.

MEDIEVAL ENGLAND: THE SETTING OF THE TIMES

Medieval is the adjective for the Middle Ages, the thousand years stretching from the end of the ancient world to the rebirth of much of the ancient ethos in the Renaissance era, roughly the 400s to the 1400s. The Anglo-Saxon period falls into this period, but because this was such a unique era in British history it has been treated separately from the rest of medieval Britain.

The medieval era has been called the "Age of Faith," and it can be argued that never before or never since have religious beliefs so dominated the minds of people living in Western civilization. It was an epoch when great cathedrals were erected; when new religious orders were founded; when friars, monks, nuns, monasteries and convents were prominent everywhere; when all those who taught at the universities were in holy orders; and when the church had the responsibility to run the hospitals and welfare systems.

Works of faith were only one side of the medieval world. Incessant warfare among armed kings, nobles, knights and retainers added chronic notes of violence and instability. Theologians regarded human sinfulness as the cause of this strife. Medieval kings tended to be weak, unless they were particularly able men. The reason for this was that, under the feudal system, medieval kings were bound in contractual roles with powerful lords. Because of this baronial strength, civil war was apt to flare up in medieval kingdoms when a minor came to the throne, when a particularly feeble king inherited the throne, or when the succession was disputed. Poor transportation and communication detracted from royal power as well.

The size and strength of castles attest to the power that medieval nobles possessed. Some were called "over-mighty subjects" whose domains bristled with armed retainers. The basis of noble power rested upon the possession of numerous manors, or medieval estates. Upon them worked masses of impoverished agricultural workers—peasants and serfs who made up the majority of the population. The manor, the nearby local church and the village comprised their entire world. Most were bound to the manor in some form of servile relationship.

Social mobility, exalted in contemporary democratic societies, was virtually unknown. Peasants begot peasants, craftsmen begot craftsmen and lords begot lords. Almost invariably, daughters married into families at their father's rank in society. Such was the will of God, who chose one's parents and thereby one's status in life. Those who tried to raise themselves into another order of society therefore defied God's choice. Bright, able young people had only one ladder to help them climb out of a low position in life: a career in the church. Yet, even in the church, the sons and daughters of the well-born were preferred for the higher ranks of the clergy.

Feudalism, the economic, political and social system of the age, allocated these manors and the peasants to a military elite. The manors often produced a thin economic surplus that managed to keep this elite of knights and lords well-armed and free to pursue war as a profession. The knights were specialists at war who operated, along with the lords above them, in a complex web of rights and obligations, most of which were sanctioned by the church. At best, feudalism sought to protect the church and peasants from violence; at worst, it exploited the masses so that the aristocratic sport of war could have full indulgence.

Many Romantic writers have embellished the Middle Ages. Troubadours, heroic knights, damsels in distress, mysterious prisoners in dungeons and the whole panoply of chivalry have been exalted. In actuality, the medieval period was dark and miserable for at least 95 percent of the population. Death came early to many people of all classes, and sometimes it came wholesale, in the form of a plague.

There were very few towns and consequently relatively few members of what can be called a "middle class." Town businessmen and craftsmen were strictly regulated by guilds, organizations concerned with quality and output. Believing that there were only limited markets for goods, the guilds sought to distribute shares of each market fairly. In England the wool trade was the most important middle-class operation. The lush grasses and fleecy sheep of the plains provided a raw material which they fashioned into woolen goods for home consumption as well as for the export trade to Europe.

Grim as these times were for most people, there are many striking medieval achievements of a lasting nature. Significant permanent institutions originated and evolved in England, including Parliament and the great ancient universities, Oxford and Cambridge. Parliament's development has been cited as the greatest achievement of the age because it shaped the development of the rest of English history. "England made a Parliament and her Parliament made England" is a popular saying.

CASTLES AND CATHEDRALS

Castles and cathedrals are the two most significant types of medieval buildings; castles reveal the warlike, struggling nature of the era while the cathedrals demonstrate its soaring faith. Both types of buildings still dominate the skylines of many places in England today, and perhaps no other place in Europe can boast such an intense concentration of these structures.

While cathedrals are constantly being restored and are still functioning, most castles have fallen into ruin. Some castles have become mere odd heaps of stone and bits of wall while others cover acres with their great walls and turrets of rough gray stone. Gone are the bright, stuccoed exteriors and lightly painted conical roofs that once flew colorful flags.

Arundel Castle, built in the 12TH century and restored in the 19TH century.

Castles were strong, defensive fortresses placed in strategic locations intended to be royal strong points. In actuality, the noblemen who were supposed to man them in the name of the king often used them against the Crown. Such castles came to represent the strength of local, feudal authority instead of the power of a distant monarch. Great, predatory noble families made castles their homes and bases of operations as they played the grand medieval sport of war. Before cannons were developed, a well-stocked and well-garrisoned castle could hold out against lengthy sieges.

Royal or noble power was but one kind of force in the Middle Ages. The other was spiritual. Perhaps there is no better way to sense this medieval power than to stand in the middle of one of its grand and glorious cathedrals and then view it from a distance. Each is unique and still serves as the source of ardent pride for local people, just as they did over five hundred years ago. Amazingly, medieval cathedrals still dominate the skylines of British cities amidst this century's modern high rises. Even though our age may take massiveness in architecture for granted, the size and grandeur of ancient cathedrals remain breathtaking.

Medieval cathedrals become even more amazing when the society that created them is contemplated. Since most medieval people were peasants living near the subsistence level on manors, how did this society muster enough social energy to construct edifices on such a magnificent scale? As with Stonehenge, cathedrals reveal the overwhelming, compelling force of religion in human life.

The medieval view of life on earth for most people was grim: Life was expected to be short and difficult, filled with toil, pain, disease, and death. The specter of starvation or plague or mysterious fevers was never far from thought. But life in the

Lincoln Cathedral, completed in the 13TH century.

world to come, in heaven, would be glorious; and, in a cathedral, medieval people could catch a glimpse of their future salvation. Magnificent cathedrals brought a little bit of heaven's majesty down to earth, and believers could be transfixed by awe and wonder at the color, artistry and music contained in these soaring edifices.

Cathedrals enabled heaven and earth to touch. Each cathedral was rooted in the earth, in the middle of masses of graves. The dead were buried one on top of the other in nearby grounds, under the cathedral, and within the cathedral walls. The remains of many important people were placed in richly carved sarcophagi in prominent places along the cathedral aisles. All around the dead flowed the living: all those who frequented the cathedral. A variety of lavish carvings and statues of people and creatures—some saintly, some wicked, and some ordinary—celebrated the living. Above, towers and spires reached skyward, seeming to touch heaven. In sum, cathedrals represented the dead, the living and life after death. What could be more important to medieval people than to put their concept of the universe into physical form and allow these sublime edifices to signify both their worship of God and their perceived relationship with Him?

Despite the uniqueness of every cathedral, there are some basic similarities. Each was built in the shape of a cross, with the east end pointing towards Jerusalem, and each served as the base for the jurisdiction, or diocese, of a bishop. All of the cathedrals were built slowly and painstakingly, often over several centuries. Salisbury Cathedral is something of an exception, as it was erected in a relatively short period of time—in just one century! These cathedrals were, of course, Roman Catholic edifices originally. It wasn't until the 16TH century that they

31

became cathedrals of the Church of England, or Anglican cathedrals. Many of them sustained some damage, destruction and remodeling from the more zealous Protestants thereafter. Additional damage has come from the air pollution of the 20TH century.

SOME FAMOUS MEDIEVAL KINGS
AND CONSTITUTIONAL DEVELOPMENTS

In many ways the Norman Conquest was a blessing in disguise for English history. It imposed a strong, unified kingdom on England at a time in European history when kingdoms tended to be weak and fragmented. Internal anarchy from warlike barons was much more of a danger to civilization in the Middle Ages than effective royal rule. Therefore the tight kingdom established by the Norman Conquest provided considerable peace and order, an environment in which important English institutions could evolve gradually.

It took an able monarch to run this strong kingdom. Medieval kings after William I varied in quality from the awful to the magnificent. Several very able English rulers were followed by inept sons. Able kings could apply justice and curb baronial anarchy—extremely important tasks in the Middle Ages. It helped to look strong and brave, and making a show out of magnificent armor, clothes and jewelry was useful to impress royal majesty upon the barons, who were often rude, ambitious and well-armed. They took advantage of princes who came to the throne too young, not very intelligent, or as homosexuals.

Since medieval political history is such a tangled skein, presenting just the minimum number of rulers might be the most

A romantic 19ᵀᴴ century depiction of what a medieval king was supposed to be: Richard the Lionhearted in front of Parliament.

helpful approach. The most outstanding and well-known kings, along with their main achievements, are worth considering:

Henry II (1154-1189) was a vigorous, able monarch who made dramatic improvements in the legal system. Henry II was the first of a line of kings called Plantagenet, whose inheritance connected the English throne with numerous provinces in France. These Plantagenet kings ruled over an Anglo-French area that was called the Angevin Empire, from 1154 to 1399.

Henry II was married to Eleanor of Aquitaine, one of the most famous women of the Middle Ages. The couple had quarrelsome sons, well-depicted in the play and film *The Lion in Winter*. Henry II was also the king in the film *Becket*.

Henry II's greatest achievements were in the fields of law and administration. He created permanent institutions designed to protect England from the disintegrating forces of baronial power. Then as now, men fought over land, wealth, authority and power. Henry's aim was to curb violence by bringing struggles out of the battlefields and into the courts. In particular, he sought to bring cases that existed on the manors out of the baronial courts and into the royal courts, where the overmighty subjects could not intimidate and control freemen. The problem was that he could not do it all himself. Therefore he arranged for royal judges to represent him and go on regular circuits around the country. These "itinerant justices" wore robes of royal red and dispensed justice in the name of the monarch, as they do today. They worked with the local sheriffs, coroners and justices of the peace—all offices filled by local persons who were acting upon what has been seen as the important medieval practice of "self-government at the king's command."

These judges came from the Curia Regis, the king's Small Council, a group of able, literate men who met regularly and handled the day-to-day business of government. The Curia Regis was the most effective part of the king's Great Council, a feudal body which brought together the great landowners and leading churchmen. There was also an elaborate bureau to handle finances called the Exchequer, named for the checkered table cloth used for tallying sums. Receipts were provided in the form of one-half of notched sticks.

Royal jurisdiction was enlarged by the use of writs, which originally were purchasable royal commands to open cases in royal courts, and by assizes, or meetings of the king and his lords to declare what the law was. In Henry II's day, the law was not derived from legislation. According to the early medieval concept, all good law was old law and merely had to be discovered. Nevertheless, discoveries through assizes actually did enlarge the common law, which was based upon precedents, customs and traditions rather than a code. It was named as such because it was common to all of England.

The jury system also emerged more strongly during Henry's reign. It can be traced back to the sworn inquests, or investigations, carried out by the Norman conquerors. Juries were drawn from twelve local freemen, the kind of people who would know the land and the customs of a given locality. At first the juries just gave what was called "the opinion of the countryside," and the royal judge decided upon the verdict. Henry introduced what we today call the Grand Jury, to indict or speak against those who might be guilty of major crimes. Petty juries in Henry's day dealt mostly with property disputes, but their role would grow in subsequent centuries.

The court of the King's Bench. The red-robed judges are in the rear, the prisoners are in the foreground.

The reputation of this dynamic king was forever stained by his implication in the assassination of Thomas á Becket, an old friend whom Henry had appointed Archbishop of Canterbury. Disputes over the privileges of churchmen, in particular their right to be tried in their own church courts, led to bitterness between the two men. In exasperation, Henry blurted, "Will no one rid me of this turbulent priest?" in the presence of four armed knights who rode off to Canterbury to butcher the Archbishop with their swords. Henry said he did not mean what he said and did penance thereafter, but strong suspicion of his guilt has lingered to the present day.

Henry was succeeded by Richard I (1189-1199), who is known as Richard the Lionhearted. He spent only a short period of his reign in England because he devoted himself to the Crusades and other adventures abroad. Robin Hood was supposed to have been active when Richard was away. Actually, the historical existence of this legendary outlaw who stole from the rich to give to the poor is questionable. Various scholars have placed him in three different medieval centuries and two locations.

John (1199-1216), Richard's younger brother, has gone down in history as a villain. He mismanaged foreign relations, fought unsuccessfully with the church, and arbitrarily milked everything he could from the feudal system. At the insistence of rebellious barons, he had to sign the Magna Carta in 1215, acknowledging legal limitations to royal power. This was important to ensure that England's strong monarchy would not veer towards despotism in future centuries. Magna Carta spelled out specific liberties of lords and freemen in great detail, and subsequent monarchs acknowledged the document by ratification when they ascended the throne. Through the centuries, Magna Carta was reinterpreted again and again so that eventually due process, the right to trial by jury and the right to be represented in a legislature all came to be read into the document. Magna Carta is also cited as a foundation for American freedom, particularly for the limitations placed on executive power.

Edward I (1272-1307) matched Henry II in ability and vigor. He is remembered for a thorough conquest of Wales and a failure to conquer Scotland; he also created innovations in the legal system to strengthen royal power and develop Parliament.

The origin of Parliament was a process, not an event. Historians have traced it to a dozen derivations, going all the way back to Anglo-Saxon folk meetings in the forests of Germany. No sweeping decree created it, and no revolution caused it to appear. It just gradually grew from the Great Council of medieval kings. At first it began as a meeting of the king with his great feudal magnates, church leaders and royal officials to talk over important matters. Sometimes early Parliaments functioned as a court. The word "Parliament" derives from the French verb "parler," meaning "to speak."

Edward regularly added what was called "the representative element," non-noble leaders from the towns and countryside. While each of the barons and bishops was summoned by name on a special writ, towns or boroughs were asked to send two leading townsmen to represent all of them. Similarly, two knights of the shire were to be chosen by property-holding freemen and were to represent the whole of each rural county. What is interesting and significant is that two houses developed, one for the lords and the other for knights and burgesses. Since knights and burgesses were officially non-noble, they were commoners at law, hence the name "House of Commons." Henceforth Parliament would always consist of three parts: crown, lords and commons. While other countries had feudal

King Edward I in Parliament from a 16ᵀᴴ century illustration. The King sits with his archbishops and royal officers. Leading clergy and noblemen sit on the benches.

39

representative bodies, they remained the strongholds of the nobility and decayed in modern times. England's Parliament became a vital organ of government because of the addition of the "representative element" which enabled the body to speak for and bind the whole realm.

Parliament was at first a tool of royal authority. Kings called it and dismissed it whenever they wished. In Edward I's reign, the main function of Parliament was to help the monarch govern by amplifying the regal voice. When Parliament spoke, one voice declared the wishes of the king and all of his subjects. Moreover, it was used to spread his views as well as to gather information and petitions from all over the realm. Only later on, in the 17TH century, did the House of Commons dare to challenge monarchical authority.

Legislation and raising taxes are functions central to Parliament today. In Edward's time, the process of "amending the common law by statute," or legislation, was just beginning. The initiative rested with the king and his council who instructed both houses. Edward confirmed Magna Carta's principle that extraordinary taxation was only to be levied with the consent of the whole realm, and that came to mean Parliament. Much later on, Parliamentarians learned to curb royal power by using their power to grant or withhold taxation.

Henry V (1413-1422) had a short but glorious reign. He fought the numerically superior French in famous campaigns across the Channel with dash and heroism—achievements celebrated by Shakespeare in the popular play named after this monarch.

Richard III (1483-1485), thanks in part to his treatment by Shakespeare, is considered one of the worst villains in English history—a vicious and greedy usurper responsible for murdering two little princes in the Tower of London. Debate still simmers over just how evil or misjudged this monarch actually was. Richard III was defeated at the hands of a challenger who became Henry VII, founder of the Tudor dynasty.

SOME FAMOUS MEDIEVAL STRUGGLES AND THE END OF THE MIDDLE AGES

From the time of Henry II onwards, England's line of Plantagenet kings had extensive holdings in France and claims to the French throne. Their possessions on both sides of the English Channel were called the Angevin Empire. Holding onto French land and claims became a costly preoccupation for English medieval kings because long and sporadic struggles with France ensued. These conflicts are termed the Hundred Years' War, lasting from around 1337 to 1453. In these struggles England won grand battles, such as Agincourt, but eventually lost the war. Losing meant being stripped of nearly all French territory, a turn of events which was beneficial for the future development of the English monarchy. At one stage, Joan of Arc emerged to resist the English as either a "saintly" or "mad" warrior, depending on one's point of view.

In the 15TH century, the descendants of the Plantagenets disputed among themselves as they sought to capture the throne, aided and abetted by rival factions of powerful nobles. These struggles, lasting from 1455 to 1485 and involving seven monarchs and an elaborate, tangled genealogy, were called the Wars of the Roses. One faction, the House of York, was associated with the white rose, and the red rose was attributed to the rival House of Lancaster. Incidentally, the actual name of the

41

The Battle of Agincourt in 1415, a great victory of Henry V.

war was bestowed by later historians, not by contemporaries. The Lancastrians won when Henry VII ascended the throne in 1485; but he calmed the dynastic rivalry considerably by marrying the heiress of the other side, Elizabeth of York. Through their son, Henry VIII, both factions were united.

Medieval civilization waned throughout Europe in the 15TH century. The widespread disaster of the 14TH century, the Black Plague, contributed immensely to this phenomenon. This highly infectious disease was spread by rats and their fleas rather swiftly during the Hundred Years' War, when armies roved over devastated areas containing malnourished populations. Eventually, England was one of the most hard-hit areas, losing up to one-half of the population. The effect on the manorial system and feudalism was profound. A shortage of peasants meant that lords sought to retain them by offering to take money payments instead of service on their lands. Some peasants rose against oppressive rents, the most massive rebellion occurring in 1381 when a huge number marched on London. Their leader, Wat Tyler, was killed in a dramatic confrontation with the city's authorities and the king himself.

There was also a popular movement against the exactions, worldliness and doctrines of the Catholic Church, led by John Wycliffe. His followers were called Lollards, and they foreshadowed the Protestantism of the future, calling for simpler services in English.

So-called "bastard feudalism" replaced crumbling manorial obligations as the Middle Ages waned. Powerful lords hired armed retainers, small private armies dressed in particular identifying colors. Future kings would have the task of disestablishing these forces before they could apply law and order— a task accomplished by the first monarchs of the Tudor dynasty.

Just when the Middle Ages came to an end is subject to interpretation. Americans tend to use the date 1492, the year when Columbus discovered the New World. Germans often cite 1517, the date when Martin Luther dramatically challenged the universal medieval church in the West. The English are likely to select 1485, the beginning of the Tudor dynasty, or the 1530s, the decade when Henry VIII's English nation was declared sovereign over the church.

The Middle Ages came to an end first in Italy. During the Italian Renaissance, the ancient world was rediscovered and appreciated, and the Italian city-states functioned as sovereign nations in miniature. It would take almost two centuries before northern Europe, including England, enjoyed its own version of the Renaissance.

HENRY VII AND THE ESTABLISHMENT OF THE TUDOR DYNASTY

As the medieval age of faith and feudalism symbolized by cathedrals and castles gradually faded into the early modern period in Europe during the 16TH century, the House of Tudor arrived on the throne in 1485. The Tudors included some of the most magnificent and brilliant English rulers of all time, and their resplendent age is appreciated today for its color and romance, as well as for its rich contributions to English theater and literature. It was also a time when many women played major roles in history, both in England and abroad. Overall, it was the time when the Renaissance came into full flower.

Many courses in American history begin with Tudor times because this is when English ships laid claim to the New World

Henry VII, the first of the Tudors.

and when English monarchs tried to colonize Virginia for the first time.

This magnificent century in English history actually began inauspiciously when the clever Henry VII barely managed to grasp the Crown during the last major round of the Wars of the Roses. His campaign was one of the most reckless gambles in history, but he defeated King Richard III, the last king of the House of York, at the closely fought Battle of Bosworth in 1485. William Shakespeare's pen gave Richard III an evil portrayal in plays enjoyed by his Tudor enemies. One memorable scene at Bosworth has Richard's crown rolling under a bush as he pleads for a mount: "A horse, a horse, my kingdom for a horse!"

Since England had eight monarchs in as many decades, few predicted that Henry would be around for many years. Henry's hereditary claim to the throne was rather dubious, since he descended from the fairly ordinary Welsh family of Tudor and had thin Lancastrian royal blood. Yet, he was able to improve the chances of establishing a Tudor dynasty by marrying the most prominent Yorkist heiress, Elizabeth of York. This guaranteed that all subsequent Tudors would have a blend of the red rose and the white rose in their ancestry.

The most compelling initial argument for his success was that he possessed the Crown by force. He was able to wear it until he died because he may have been the most clever monarch ever to sit upon the English throne. He squashed the plots of his rivals and carefully husbanded royal wealth, knowing that a full treasury meant the possibility of putting armies in the field if necessary. Like many wise rulers, he preferred negotiation to costly warfare, so he avoided military activity as much as possible. His subjects surely yearned for peace and the end of baronial strife as much as he did. Since so

Ruins of Fountains Abbey, Yorkshire.

47

many nobles had been killed in the Wars of the Roses, Henry VII was able to create new nobles whose loyalty to the House of Tudor could be depended upon. Henry picked good advisors and administrators as well, often selecting individuals who had skill and intelligence even if they did not have an impressive ancestry. Together, Henry and his royal council curtailed the overmighty subjects with fines and confiscations. While he was not a glamorous or showy monarch, he was able to pass on a solid, solvent, and peaceful kingdom to his son who, unlike his thrifty, careful father, was indeed a glamorous showman.

HENRY VIII AND THE ENGLISH REFORMATION

Henry VIII has always been controversial. Who was the real Henry VIII? Was he the charming, talented Renaissance prince, or the vicious, egotistical tyrant? In order to secure a legitimate heir, he married six women. He beheaded two of them and divorced two of them; one died in childbirth and one outlived him. Along the way, he opened the floodgates of the Reformation in England by breaking with the Roman Catholic Church and becoming the leader of the Church of England, which more or less kept the same buildings and personnel. While he did destroy the monasteries, a Protestant tactic, much else in the church remained similar to Roman Catholic practice. The American equivalent of the Church of England is the Episcopal Church. Episcopalians often have considerable difficulty dealing with the foundation of their denomination: Henry VIII's religious innovations. Today, the topic continues to elicit sprightly discussions.

Henry VIII, a famous portrait by Hans Holbein.

Henry was welcomed and praised in his youth, a time when he was robust and fun-loving and a far cry from his later years of tyranny. While young, he exceeded his subjects in brain and brawn. A six-foot-four-inch athlete, he participated in many sports including archery, tilting, tennis and hunting. He was also a clever theologian, musician and patron of the new learning. After his father's reign of thrift and caution, courtiers were pleased to see a monarch who loved to dress well, give parties and enjoy food, drink and women.

Henry's first queen, Catherine of Aragon, a serious and devout Spanish princess, gave birth to his daughter Mary, who later ruled as Mary I or "Bloody Mary." No other children were likely to be forthcoming from the aging Catherine, and anxieties rose about the need for a legitimate male heir to prevent a relapse into the bloody civil wars of noble factions that had preceded the Tudors. Indeed, the new peace and prosperity of the Tudor dynasty hung upon the thread of a single life, that of Henry VIII. At this time, the prospect of rule by a queen was deemed dangerous because it was feared that a female ruler would be dominated by a male faction or be unstable and incapable of ruling on account of her gender. (This was truly before the time of Elizabeth I!)

Henry's desperate need for a legitimate male heir coincided with the eruption of his great passion for Anne Boleyn, a woman at court from a not particularly high-ranking family. The relationship between Henry and Anne became one of the most remarkable romances of all history. Unlike other women at court, Anne resisted Henry until he was willing to promise her everything, which meant marriage and a throne. Because of Henry's unbounded passion for her, he divorced Catherine of Aragon and made Anne queen. But, because of a complicated

Anne Boleyn, Henry's second wife and the mother of Elizabeth I.

international situation, the Pope did not cooperate when Henry sought an annulment of his marriage to Catherine. In the past, many monarchs had been accommodated by the Papacy in even more flagrant attempts to set aside unproductive marriages.

The person charged with arranging an annulment was the notorious and brilliant Cardinal Wolsey, Henry's colorful right-hand man. Wolsey was an upstart, the son of an Ipswich butcher, but he was always a hard and faithful worker for the Crown. Henry VIII rewarded him with the highest offices of state and church. With the fortune that such preferment brought, Wolsey was able to build the magnificent complex of Hampton Court Palace just outside of London, a place that still seems to be haunted by him and by his monarch. Despite his skill and intrigues abroad, Wolsey was unable to achieve the annulment of Henry's marriage and he was promptly dismissed. Always Henry's creature, Wolsey's power and prestige vanished. He died in disgrace, just short of the executioner's axe.

If the Catholic Church would not grant an annulment, it would have to be done in an English church court. Henry was in a hurry, since Anne was pregnant with what he hoped would be the male heir destined to give stability to the Tudor dynasty. But, the baby was a girl, Elizabeth.

Henry's great passion for Anne Boleyn soon changed from love to hate, and Anne was executed. Henry's next wife, Jane Seymour, died in childbirth, but the child was the long-awaited male heir who became Edward VI. Henry had no other children by his subsequent wives: Anne of Cleves, Catherine Howard and Catherine Parr. The fate of these ladies is recalled in the schoolboy's rhyme: "Divorced, beheaded, died; divorced, beheaded, survived." They made up a total of three Catherines, two Annes, and one Jane.

During the time that Henry was becoming middle-aged, overweight, increasingly unpleasant and arbitrary, the Anglican Church continued to develop separate from Rome. Henry insisted that Catholic doctrine and practices be maintained, such as the nature of the Mass and the celibacy of the clergy. Yet at the same time he introduced Protestant innovations: English was introduced in the church services through the use of Archbishop Cranmer's elegant prayer books and an English Bible. The destruction of monasteries, convents and abbeys were definitely Protestant innovations. It was true that many of these religious houses had indeed fallen away from their medieval ideals, but Henry closed them all, pensioned off the religious persons who cooperated, and executed the few who resisted.

These church properties came with considerable land, and Henry temporarily enriched the Crown by selling them. The landed classes obtained land at bargain prices and thereby acquired a strong economic reason for supporting what has come to be known as the Henrician Reformation. Throughout England, magnificent old monastic church buildings were looted, stripped of their lead roofs and even used as stone quarries. Their ruins dot the countryside today, testimony to the zeal of Henry's agents to despoil the church. Elsewhere in Europe, other Protestant leaders acted similarly. Medieval monasticism only survived intact in southern, Catholic Europe.

As Henry took steps to sever England from the international church he declared that his kingdom was an empire unto itself, sovereign and supreme over all things in church and state. This was a leap forward for nationalism, and it was not achieved without the great amplification of the king's policies through Parliament in the form of statutes. Of course,

Henry VIII's Parliaments were rubber stamps for this powerful, willful king. The English Reformation was pushed through from the top, but the very fact that Parliament was central to the process was significant. His father had not used Parliament much, and some people thought that it would quietly ossify like so many other medieval institutions. The Reformation breathed new life into the old institution, reaffirming that the consent of the whole realm was manifest when it passed important legislation.

Henry was ruthless when faced with opposition. Like the other clever Tudors, he used the executioner's axe sparingly, and only after scrupulous trials on trumped up charges. How he treated those who opposed the Henrician Reformation is a case in point. Those who wanted advanced Protestant innovations, say along Lutheran lines, were burned at the stake for heresy. All Roman Catholics who objected to the state being put over the church in England were decapitated for treason. The argument was that the Roman Catholics put loyalty to a foreign ruler, the Pope, ahead of loyalty to their sovereign king. The most famous Englishman to suffer this fate was the cultured, talented and highly principled Thomas More, a man who would not take an oath to validate what he saw as a usurpation of the realm of the spirit by secular authority.

THE LITTLE TUDORS

After Henry VIII died in 1547, he was succeeded by his only son, Edward VI, who was still a child, and a sickly one at that. He died at sixteen after six years as a manipulated child king.

During Edward's brief reign, the Church of England took a turn towards greater Protestant innovations.

Henry's two daughters followed. The eldest, Mary I, was a tragic figure and a pious Roman Catholic like her mother, who put her religious principles above prudence and all else. She became notorious for burning Protestants at the stake at the notorious "Smithfield Fires." Although of kindly temperament when not motivated by religious fanaticism, Mary has gone down in history as "Bloody Mary." Her main goal was to bring England back into the fold of Catholic nations, and to this end she married the most powerful Catholic monarch in Europe, King Philip II of Spain. To her disappointment, she could not become pregnant and thus lost the opportunity to impose a line of Catholic heirs on England.

Today, the fury of religious persecution of the 16TH and 17TH centuries is hard to comprehend. What was perceived to be at risk in those times was salvation itself. Heretics led the innocent children of God astray and perverted God's teachings. They were eliminated to protect the virtuous from being led down the path to eternal damnation—cut out of society the way a surgeon cuts cancerous tissue from a patient. Unfortunately, each side saw the other side as heretical; Catholics identified Protestants as heretics and vice versa. Many Protestants compounded matters by finding other kinds of Protestant heretics. Although the 20TH century has seen its own horrors in punishing heretics, the difference is that modern heresy involves nationalism, ethnicity and beliefs in economic systems.

"Bloody Mary" is sometimes confused with Mary, Queen of Scots, who was also a Catholic, but a member of the Stuart family instead of the Tudor dynasty. Mary, Queen of Scots, played her role in history during the reign of Elizabeth I.

An allegory of the Tudor Succession. In this imaginary painting designed to instruct, "Bloody Mary" emerges on the left with Philip II and Mars, the God of War; on the right, Elizabeth brings the goddesses of peace and plenty.

THE ELIZABETHAN AGE: 1558-1603

As Henry VIII's second daughter, Elizabeth's early years were traumatic; her mother, Anne Boleyn, had been beheaded not long after her birth and she was in an extremely precarious position at the court of her half-sister, Mary I. Once Mary died childless, Elizabeth ruled for one of the most colorful and dramatic half-centuries in English history, from 1558 to 1603.

This was a golden age, a time of spiritual, cultural and economic expansion and achievement. Population, commerce and wealth continued to flourish. Shakespeare and other talented Englishmen enriched the increasingly flexible English language with their magnificent works. Artists fashioned portraits, silverware, miniatures, and jewelry on an unprecedented scale. Fine examples of Elizabethan architecture grace many parts of England to this day.

This was also a time of danger and heroism for England and her Queen. This golden age was played out against a backdrop of immense international tension as the Catholic Counter-Reformation gained strength on the Continent. Protestant England was confronted by hostile Catholic states, the strongest of which was Spain. English "sea dogs," acting as semi-pirates, found adventure on the oceans harrying Spanish commerce. Meanwhile, Jesuits worked hard to reconvert Protestant Europe, and extremists made assassination a constant threat for Elizabeth. If she died, Mary, Queen of Scots, a flamboyant and attractive Catholic ruler, was next in line to the English throne. When Mary fled from hostile factions in Scotland to England, Elizabeth made her a captive; and finally, when Mary was implicated in plots against Elizabeth's life, the English monarch reluctantly allowed her execution to take place, pretending that she had been tricked into giving consent.

Shakespeare's birthplace at Stratford-upon-Avon.

This deed launched the Spanish Armada against England in 1588, a great invasion fleet sent by King Philip II of Spain because he now claimed the throne of England for himself. Spain was the greatest power of the 16TH century, achieving near hegemony, or control, on the Continent. The courageous English navy and a fortunate storm combined to wreck the Spanish fleet. This was the first but not the last time that England faced the challenge of a dominant European power and defeated it. France and Germany would share the same fate in future centuries.

Despite the prejudices against women rulers, Elizabeth governed skillfully and magnificently. One of her main achievements was settling religious discord through a broad, comprehensive church settlement. She was beset by radical Protestants on the left and determined Catholics on the right. Her solution was to create a broad Church of England that went right down the middle. She sought to pull in as many Protestants and Catholics as possible. Disputatious issues, such as the nature of communion or Mass, were deliberately left vague in Elizabethan prayer books in order to be inoffensive to as many people as possible. Elizabeth was cautious about her own religious views. She was probably a skeptic. She did not like religious disputes, nor did she wish to pursue those who kept the old Catholic faith. Nevertheless, she did execute well over one hundred Catholics for treason, most of them priests who were illegally operating against her in England.

Although Elizabeth never married, she constantly presented herself as an advantageous match to a number of European rulers and princes, dangling the possibility of marriage as a powerful diplomatic ploy. She did have a strong romantic attachment to one of her subjects, the Earl of Leicester. How far she carried on her dalliance with him is impossible for

Elizabeth in her "Armada Portrait," celebrating the great English victory over the Spanish fleet in 1588.

historians to say. When Leicester's wife died under suspicious circumstances, Elizabeth became convinced that she should never marry her favorite because of a public outrage. Elizabeth "flirted" with many men at court, and they responded by flattering her lavishly. It was all a game, as courtiers rose and fell. Yet Elizabeth did not govern her kingdom with the colorful, witty men who amused her at court. Instead, she chose dedicated, talented ministers who worked for her throughout their careers, men who could put up with her sporadic outbursts of temper.

Like her grandfather, Henry VII, Elizabeth was frugal. She spent lavishly on only one luxury, her elaborate dresses. She was also like her father, Henry VIII—adept at showmanship and seeking public adulation from her subjects. She did, however, share the keen intelligence of both of these forebears. She worked hard at all hours, tending to sleep briefly when she wanted to, and eating at irregular hours—habits which must have vexed her ministers. From time to time she was troubled by what was then called melancholia and now called depression. She died husbandless and childless, but revered by nearly all of her subjects.

Elizabeth was most skilled in handling her Parliaments. She was gracious and flirtatious, particularly with members of the House of Commons who responded with bursts of eloquent patriotism. In times of emergency, they were usually quite willing to vote subsidies, the term for extra taxes, for the Queen's government. She certainly needed them, as she was a poor monarch in a rich state. The Crown had been set up with various sources of revenue in the Middle Ages, but inflation eroded the value of these ancient taxes and grants.

Regardless of her need to coax subsidies from them, Elizabeth would not allow Parliamentarians to concern themselves with three areas that she regarded as strictly prerogative, or royal, concerns: foreign policy, including her possible marriage, the church establishment, and the question of succession. When radicals in Parliament sought to broach these matters, Elizabeth reprimanded them. Despite such squabbles, on the whole the Elizabethan era left a harmoniousness in government and society, a recollection of a time when Crown, Lords and Commons cooperated magnificently. Her golden age became a very fond memory in the discordant century that followed.

THE EARLY STUARTS AND THE ORIGINS OF THE CIVIL WAR

The Stuart era can be easily arranged chronologically. It covers roughly the 17TH century, and Stuart kings can be remembered by this string of letters: J-C-O-C-J, for the reigns of James I (1603-1625), Charles I (1625-1649), Charles II (1660-1685), and James II (1685-1688). It helps to remember that the J's are on the outside and the C's are on the inside and that two I's come first, followed by two II's. The "O" in the middle stands for Oliver Cromwell, who ruled during most of the interregnum ("times without kings"), which lasted from 1649 until the Restoration of 1660. During the interregnum, there were two republican forms of government, called the "Commonwealth" and the "Protectorate." Both were dependent upon Cromwell's military power.

The central dramatic event in the Stuart century was the English Civil War, a struggle which pitted royalists, called Cavaliers, against Parliamentarians, who were often called Roundheads because of the shape of their helmets. These struggles, fought from 1642 to 1648, had three basic, interrelated causes: the arbitrary rule of the Stuart kings, the rise of the gentry, and the spread of Puritanism.

The ineffective rule of the first two Stuart kings contributed significantly to the outbreak. James I, for whom the King James version of the Bible is named, was a pretentious Scot. He was the son of Mary, Queen of Scots, but he was raised as a Protestant. He was reasonably successful as King James VI in Scotland, but when he became James I, King of England, he proved to be arrogant and ineffective, lacking an appreciation of English law and customs. While Elizabeth I was a difficult act to follow, James made matters worse by becoming overly attached to ambitious male favorites. Moreover, he was not a prepossessing monarch, with his spindly legs, bulging eyes, lisped Scots accent, and tendency to drink too much. At least, he did unite the two nations of England and Scotland during his personal rule. The term "Jacobean" refers to his reign because it derives from the Hebrew name for James, which is Jacob. He also gave his name to the first permanent English settlement in America, Jamestown, founded in 1607.

His son, Charles I, is considered a saint and martyr in the view of some people, and a would-be tyrant in the eyes of others. He was a royal figure whose temperament did not lend itself well to the task of ruling. In his private life he was cultured, usually gentle and pleasant, and a good husband and father; but, as a ruler, he was often incompetent or irresolute, and at times blind and stubborn. He strove for strong royal government in England along the lines of Continental royal absolutism. He, along with his father, thought that strong royal rule was "modern" and that the old English law and surviving medieval institutions, such as Parliament, were old-fashioned.

Charles I, a famous portrait by Van Dyck.

In order to subvert Parliament's power of the purse, he attempted to raise money by various dubious means so that he could dispense with new money grants from Parliament. He avoided calling Parliament for eleven years. This so-called "Eleven Years' Tyranny," from 1629 to 1641, led to one conflict after another with influential groups in society. Charles insisted that royal judges give verdicts sought by the Crown, and he contended that persons could be arrested simply because the king wanted them in jail. These policies, thought by Charles and his ministers to be in line with the latest royal policies on the Continent, went against the grain of a long tradition of Parliamentary government and the exercise of the common law. His opponents pointed out his violation of the ancient English constitution, and they raised the cry of "no taxation without representation."

The English gentry, or country gentlemen, presented the most forceful and effective opposition to these Stuart kings. The gentry comprised a class unique to England which was powerful in the countryside and in local government and highly represented in the House of Commons. These were the proud, well-educated, active and public-spirited landowners who fell just below the aristocracy and therefore were considered "non-noble" (although they did fashion coats of arms for themselves). As a group, they descended from the medieval knights. Even so, the gentry were constantly reinforced by prosperous landowners with pretensions but more questionable pedigrees. Many wealthy merchants, lawyers, doctors and prosperous yeomen held hopes that their sons or grandsons, installed on purchased estates, could eventually be regarded as country gentlemen with "Esquire" tacked after their names. Great Virginia families, such as the Madison or Washington families, lived lives akin to those of the English gentry.

*The country gentleman in the 17TH century with advice to foster his
ideal behavior.*

In the early 17TH century significant numbers of the gentry took radical positions in politics and religion. These were the gentlemen who opposed the Crown vigorously and became Puritans. From their bastion of power in the House of Commons, they were eventually able to break the power of the Stuart kings and limit the power of the British monarchy for generations to come.

Religious wars on the continent during this century usually involved Catholics against Protestants. England was unique in that two varieties of Protestants fought each other: the Anglicans coming out for the King and the Puritans coming out for the Parliamentarians. In fact, many of the country gentry in Parliament were devout Puritans, such as Oliver Cromwell. But just who were the Puritans?

Puritans were Bible-based Protestants who were inspired by the French theologian, John Calvin, who sought to "purify" the Anglican Church by making it more Protestant and less Catholic. This meant emphasizing sermons and the Bible more than ritual, making the physical appearance of the church plain and simple, and reforming all of society according to a Puritan interpretation of God's will. These matters were crucial and had to be carried out with zeal, and at any cost. Puritans saw themselves as a spiritual elite predestined for salvation—activists who were God's instruments in this fallen world. There was also a democratic impulse in Puritanism because all men were seen as equal in the eyes of God, and they championed a priesthood of all believers. In congregations, the Bible was studied and discussed with great passion, and with feelings that were readily transferred into politics. Backed by what they believed was the will of God, Puritans dared to draw their swords even against an ungodly but anointed king.

Throughout the 17TH century Puritans left England in numbers that were to multiply in the open lands of the New World and give American Protestantism a decidedly Calvinist emphasis. The influence of Puritanism has been felt many times in American history, through such movements as temperance, prohibition, and laws concerning sexual behavior. The old-fashioned, strict, and sober American work ethic can also be attributed to Puritan heritage.

In the early 17TH century Puritans campaigned to change the Anglican Church by eliminating all elements associated with Roman Catholicism, in particular reliance upon bishops. James I and Charles I staunchly resisted them and promoted high church Anglicanism instead. The Puritans suspected these kings of Catholic sympathies, particularly when Charles married a French Catholic princess.

Eventually, a Scottish uprising over religious matters forced King Charles I to call Parliament because he could not suppress the Scots without extra funds. The Parliament of 1640 became the famous "Long Parliament," which was not officially dismissed until 1660, though its personnel and practices changed many times during the civil war.

The early legislation of the Long Parliament, designed to curtail arbitrary power, was enduring. Charles could not use the royal veto against these laws because he was in a crisis and out of funds. Henceforth British monarchs had to summon Parliament regularly, eliminate arbitrary courts, use common law courts and discontinue all forms of illegal, non-Parliamentary taxation.

Violence between the king and the angry Puritanical gentlemen in the House of Commons was triggered by two events. First, the Irish rose in a vicious rebellion in 1641. An army was raised to put them down, but Parliament did not trust Charles with a large army, so they tried to control it themselves. Second, Charles, exasperated with his more outspoken opponents, sought to arrest five members in the House of Commons in early 1642, an unprecedented arbitrary action. Thereafter conciliation was out of the question as both sides raised armies.

THE ENGLISH CIVIL WAR

Deciphering who fought whom in the English Civil War is a complex issue. Families were often divided, as they often were in border states during the American Civil War. Charles tended to have the support of the more traditional and agrarian areas in the north and west. Parliament controlled the south and east, including wealthy London with its fleet.

Royalists and Parliamentarians fought hard for control of England. The battles of Edgehill, Naseby and Marston Moor are among the bloodiest ever held on English soil. In the end, the wealth and numbers from the southern part of England— London especially—defeated the Royalists.

Cavalry was the supreme arm in the Civil War and at first the Cavaliers, so accustomed to the hunt, had an initial advantage (similar to the Confederate horsemen in the American Civil War). Soon Parliament organized and trained powerful units of horsemen who were mostly zealous Puritans. Their discipline and treatment of civilians was excellent, but they fought their enemy with an almost fanatical passion.

The most skilled commander of Puritan cavalry had been a minor country gentleman from a place near Cambridge before discovering his military skills at the age of forty. As the war progressed he became the leader of the whole Parliamentary side and thereafter came to rule England as its Protector. This was Oliver Cromwell, who fought and governed for the "glory of God" by destroying the Almighty's enemies, or so he believed.

Cromwell has remained an important and controversial figure—someone who rarely elicits impartiality. For some he is a hero and for others he is a villain; particularly in Ireland he is thought to be the latter, where his rule was noted for its brutality and destructiveness. Many Protestants and some left-wing politicians see Cromwell as a knight in shining armor, while most Anglicans and Irish Roman Catholics depict him as a destroyer.

As the leader of the regicides, Cromwell was certainly a scourge to Charles I who lost the Civil War, was captured, and then secretly plotted to launch a second civil war. Meanwhile, Parliament had been purged of moderate members by the army. The body remaining was contemptuously called the "Rump Parliament." When the Puritans called for the execution of Charles I, "a man of blood," it was accomplished. Charles died with faith and dignity and subsequently became a saint of the Anglican Church.

A period of interregnum followed from 1649 to the Restoration of 1660. During this time Oliver Cromwell reluctantly took over the state, but he would not accept a crown for himself. Although he sought to rule with a Parliament of Puritan saints, the members were too impassioned with religious issues to govern. Things were so chaotic that for the first and only time in English history a virtual military dictatorship prevailed. Cromwell was a strong man on horseback, a type likely to emerge as ruler in times of revolutionary turmoil. Ironically, a rebellion against arbitrary rule by a king ended with the

A marble bust of Oliver Cromwell.

Cromwell's army appealing to God before a battle. This is from a 19TH century painting.

arbitrary rule of a general. Cromwell's army had more power than Charles ever dreamed of having, including the power to collect higher taxes than Charles had ever proposed. After Cromwell, militarism has had a bad reputation in Britain, and ever since, except during the World Wars, British standing armies have been small, professional and nonpolitical.

During Cromwell's rule, the House of Lords was abolished and the Anglican Church ceased to be the state church. This was a time of social upheaval, as many men and women emerged from the lower and middle ranks of society to assume new responsibilities. In addition, religious fanaticism spread. Raving zealots emerged as sects multiplied rapidly. Some were so radical in social behavior that Cromwell's soldiers were required to suppress them. There were other aspects of repression: theaters were closed, popular gambling was suppressed, and severe penalties were applied to sexual irregularities and blasphemy.

England's controversial leader during this brief period of English republicanism died in bed, bequeathing power to his son who was incompetent. Soon, some of the army generals were negotiating with the Stuart heir to the throne to restore the monarchy in an ideal, limited and constitutional form.

THE RESTORATION OF 1660 AND THE GLORIOUS REVOLUTION OF 1688

For Americans, it seems curious that a republic would be replaced with a restored monarchy in 1660. The Stuarts returned to the throne largely because royal governance was deemed normal for 17TH century society. Charles II made it easier by promising to be a limited and constitutional monarch who would obey the laws of the realm and guarantee all Englishmen their freedoms and most of the property they had expropriated during the Civil War.

Another reason for the Restoration involved a shift in attitudes of the gentry. Their role before and after the Civil War was to hold power on the land and in local government throughout England. After Cromwell's rule in mid-century, the gentry turned away from revolutionary excesses and became rather conservative. They had seen enough violence, wild experimentation, religious passion and arbitrary rule in Cromwell's time and were quite willing to welcome back a Stuart monarch and see the reestablishment of the Anglican Church and the House of Lords.

Charles II turned out to be a skillful, genial lecher. In stark contrast to the Puritan era preceding it, the Restoration was a time of hedonism—that is, a time when pleasure-seeking was primary, particularly the enjoyment of food, drink and sex. The king set an example for his subjects in hedonism, but he also played skillful games with Parliamentarians and thereby retained a fair amount of royal power. He was tolerant towards Catholics, marrying a Catholic princess from Portugal and converting from Anglicanism to Catholicism, himself, on his deathbed. During his reign some disasters befell England: the plague broke out again (1665-1666); most of London burned down in the Great Fire (1666); and the Dutch were able to inflict some defeats on Britain at sea and even sail warships up the Thames estuary (1667).

While Puritans may have thought that these events reflected the judgment of God upon a sinful city, they themselves were in great disrepute during the Restoration, thanks to

Charles II, the Stuart restored in 1660.

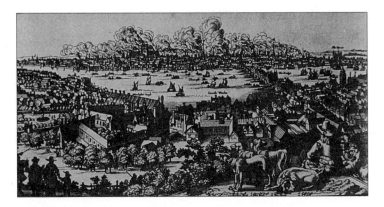

The city of London during the Great Fire of 1666.

their excesses during the Civil War. Puritans were associated with Cromwell, military rule and the fanaticism of some sects. Therefore, after Cromwell, the Puritans were a despised minority in England. Since they could no longer hope to reform the Anglican Church, they had to function outside of it; and, since groups differed from each other in terms of religious issues, they had to form several church denominations. Cromwell's followers became Congregationalists, and others became Baptists, Quakers, Presbyterians, or formed other denominations.

The defeated and despised Puritans were tolerated and called "Nonconformists" or "Dissenters" because they did not conform to the reestablished Anglican Church. Toleration of them did not mean, however, that they were free from discrimination. Religious toleration, new to European history, began in England where it operated with a rather narrow scope. Toleration merely meant that worshippers were allowed to believe whatever they wanted without persecution. Social and political discrimination against the Puritan sects lasted for over a century. For example, non-Anglicans were not supposed to hold public office or obtain degrees from Oxford or Cambridge. Barred from the centers of power, Nonconformists turned to careers in business and industry, where many became successful capitalists noted for their strict attention to detail, sobriety, and honesty. Many others took ship for the New World. England's limited toleration was enacted into law by the Toleration Act of 1689.

Since Charles had no legitimate children (although he acknowledged a swarm of illegitimate ones), his brother, James, was to succeed him. James was a man of limited ability, but what was worse was the fact that he was a devout Roman

Catholic. There was a considerable amount of controversy about James' succession, called the Exclusion Issue. It was over this issue that the first political parties clearly emerged in English history. One group of politicians was labeled Whig and another Tory—both derogatory nicknames. The Whigs wanted to exclude James from the throne, stating that a Catholic king could not govern a Protestant country. The Tories, in contrast, were willing to tolerate him, believing that hereditary right should be preeminent; besides, he was getting old and he had, at that time, only Protestant heirs. While the names of political parties would change over the next three centuries, the two-party system continued to operate.

Utilizing skillful maneuvers, Charles prevented the Whigs from excluding his brother. When he became king, James II was unable and unwilling to compromise his devout Roman Catholic faith. Foolishly, he attempted to bring the nation back into the Catholic fold by filling offices in the state and army with his co-religionists. He contemptuously suspended the laws which were designed to keep the government of England in Protestant control, and he appointed Roman Catholics to important offices despite the small number of able Catholics available to serve him. In addition, he tampered with Parliamentary elections and revoked old charters and local privileges arbitrarily.

Opposition to James' brash and unconstitutional pro-Catholic policies grew among the landowners of England. Yet most decided to wait out his reign since he was in his late fifties (which then was considered a more advanced age than it is now). James' first wife, Anne Hyde, had been a Protestant, with whom he had two Protestant daughters, Mary and Anne, his logical successors. Then an event occurred which was regarded by Catholics as something of a miracle, and by Protestants as a probable fraud:

His new wife, Mary of Modena, a Catholic, gave birth to a healthy male child who, if he lived to maturity, might guarantee a long line of Catholic monarchs for Protestant England.

The influential portions of the landed classes decided to act. They invited his eldest Protestant daughter, Mary, who was married to William of Orange of the Netherlands, to come to England to overthrow James and reign in his stead. William insisted on being co-monarch with Mary and the Parliamentarians acceded to his wishes. William was willing to assume this risky proposition because he wanted to bring England into an anti-French coalition to help save the Dutch from French aggression.

William and Mary sailed from the Netherlands sped on by what was called a "Protestant Wind" blowing from the northeast. The same gusts helped to keep James II's ships bottled up in port. Once in England, William and Mary were welcomed by their Whig and Tory supporters and they turned to face James' Catholic-led armies which suddenly dissolved before them. James fled, and was declared to have abdicated.

This set of events, a *coup d'etat*, was the much celebrated "Glorious Revolution" of 1688, which reaffirmed the limited nature of the English monarchy. It demonstrated the principle that monarchs who broke their contracts could be removed by their subjects, a point stressed by the political philosopher important on both sides of the Atlantic: John Locke. Subsequently, Americans made use of this principle in dealing with George III. The very language used to accuse James II of misdeeds against the constitution was borrowed by Americans for the Declaration of Independence. Americans also adopted almost all of the Bill of Rights, which was promulgated immediately after the Glorious Revolution. These rights are fundamental to the constitutions of both countries and demonstrate how similar both counties are in cherishing liberties and specific freedoms.

CULTURAL ACHIEVEMENTS OF THE STUART ERA AND THE LAST STUARTS

English literature and theater maintained a high reputation for creativity and richness dating from the Restoration to the end of the Stuart era. In architecture, the genius of Christopher Wren was at work. Not only did he design St. Paul's Cathedral and dozens of churches, but he also supervised the rebuilding of London after the disastrous Great Fire of 1666, which left the older parts of the city a smoldering ruin. Wren employed classical features, such as domes and columns, on structures which were strongly influenced by the Renaissance in France and Italy. This Renaissance impulse sought to incorporate the restraint, discipline and order of ancient times with a graceful, moderate style.

Some of the greatest achievements in British science belong to the latter 17TH century. At that time many talented people were inclined to turn away from the vexed topics of religion and spend their energies on the exploration of the natural world. Important advances were achieved in physics, chemistry, mathematics and anatomy. Scientists had greater opportunities to interact and encourage one another because the Royal Society, still the preeminent organization of English scientists, was founded during the Restoration. The giant among these scientists was Sir Isaac Newton, whose world view of physics lasted until the time of Einstein and whose mechanics still have many practical applications today. Together with Charles Darwin,

Newton shares the distinction of being one of the two greatest British scientists of all time.

The last of the Stuarts operated as limited monarchs within the framework of the constitution. William and Mary were followed by another of James II's Protestant daughters, Queen Anne (1702-1714). Anne bore seventeen children, all of whom died.

From the time of the Glorious Revolution onward, it was clear that powerful France, dominant on the Continent, had become a national enemy much as Spain had been in the 16TH century. Britain became involved in a series of wars against France, spanning the years 1688 to 1815, which have often been called the "second Hundred Years' War." These wars were fought on all the oceans, in North America, India, as well as on the continent of Europe. As British statesmen arranged coalitions of Continental states to fight French expansion during Queen Anne's reign, the Churchill family rose to prominence. John Churchill, a brilliant general and Winston Churchill's ancestor, became the first Duke of Marlborough as a reward for winning military glory against the French on the Continent. He also obtained a large monetary reward, enabling him to build Blenheim Palace, named for one of his greatest victories.

POLITICS IN THE GEORGIAN ERA: 1714-1789

This period takes its name from the four Georges who ruled England in the logical order of George I, II, III and IV. The last George died in 1830, but the eruption of the French Revolution in 1789 can be used to mark the coming of a new era. In

Blenheim Palace near Oxford.

addition, the Industrial Revolution, underway by the 1770s, would transform Britain for all time. Therefore, there is some logic in curtailing the Georgian period in 1789.

For the last time in British history, the landed classes, aristocracy and gentry clearly dominated society and politics. Towards the end of the century, the middle class had grown considerably both in number and importance, due largely to the expansion of trade and urban areas. By the 19TH century, the middle class would seek to break the dominance of the landed classes in politics and society. Yet, in the 18TH century, the landed classes enjoyed an unchallenged exercise of their power and relished the display of their lavish lifestyle.

The four Georges were called Hanoverians because their dynasty came from the small German province of that name. They were the closest Protestant heirs to the English throne, and ascended it only because a law of the early 18TH century permanently disqualified Roman Catholics from being crowned. Therefore, the Stuart line, in exile in France, remained disqualified even though they had a better claim by heredity. The exiled Stuarts had their strongest supporters in Scotland, the original home of the dynasty. On two occasions, in 1715 and 1745, Stuart pretenders to the English throne came back to Scotland and led rebellious forces into England. After savage fighting, the rebels were suppressed and the Stuarts were forced to flee to France once more. Termed the Jacobite Risings, these events were frightening for politicians in London as well as for the Hanoverians themselves.

Fortunately for the development of the English constitution, the first two Georges were foreign, homesick, intellectually limited, and German-speaking. As a result, the great English statesmen who sat in the House of Commons and the House of

Lords took over nearly all of the functions of the executive branch of government. In order to line up votes and influence, Parliament they passed out honors, promotions and offices in the king's name. Since the first two Georges were usually absentees in mind if not in body, English politicians arranged for appointments to ministries and jockeyed among themselves for political prominence and authority. Obviously, this system was held together by widespread bribery and corruption; but it actually worked, enabling the executive power to come from the legislature rather than from the Crown.

Political organs to manage the state evolved quietly under the weak Hanoverian Crown. These were the cabinet and the office of prime minister, components of government that facilitated the shift in ministerial responsibility from the Crown to Parliament. Operating together informally, a small group of key ministers formed the first cabinets, and the most important minister gained the title of prime minister—ironically a term of derision initially.

Invariably, these politicians had to command substantial followings in the legislature in order to be at the center of things. A minister with a following and many friends was likely to have sufficient support to push through legislation on the floor of the House of Commons and the House of Lords. Politicians became adept at piecing together workable coalitions from the supporters of various individuals. Therefore, if the whole cabinet was made up of influential men with many supporters, the prime minister had a good chance of governing effectively. Theoretically, ministers were still responsible to the king, but in actuality they became more responsible to the House of Commons. A series of leading politicians entered and left office peacefully and undramatically throughout the 18TH century.

The first prime minister was Sir Robert Walpole, a skilled manipulator of patronage and influence. Significantly, he sat in the House of Commons rather than in the House of Lords, indicating that the lower house had finally become the most important part of Parliament. Walpole's motto, "every man has his price," indicates that there was always something to offer for a vote in the House of Commons.

Later in the century, a father and son named Pitt were outstanding prime ministers. William Pitt the Elder was a great war leader of the French and Indian War (1757-1763), called the Seven Years' War in Europe. Pittsburgh, Pennsylvania, was named after him. He was sympathetic to the American cause in the era of the American Revolution. Later in life he became the Earl of Chatham and is therefore commonly referred to as Chatham. His son, William Pitt the Younger, picked up the pieces for King George III after the American Revolution and continued in office until his death in 1806 during the wars with Napoleon. William Pitt the Younger is noted for becoming prime minister at the young age of twenty-four.

The evolution of government in Georgian England was highly significant, not just for England but for the rest of the world. Today, parliamentary democracy in Europe and elsewhere features cabinets whose ministers are responsible for and come from the legislature. If they do not have legislative support, the cabinet government falls. At some point in its history, Britain served as the model for each of these representative governments where the executive is made up of leaders from the legislature.

It was a different story for the United States. The American constitution calls for a strict separation between executive and legislative power. Britain was the inspiration for this, as well.

Sir Robert Walpole presiding at an early Cabinet meeting.

Americans wanted to purify the system by ensuring that legislators could not usurp executive powers through bribery and corruption. American cabinet members are barred from seats in the legislature.

SOCIETY IN GEORGIAN ENGLAND

Just as the landed classes, the aristocracy and the gentry dominated the House of Lords and the House of Commons, respectively, the big country houses, town houses, elegant clothes, rich furnishings, and frequent travel clearly exposed the unchallenged economic and social dominance of these classes.

For part of the year most stayed on their vast estates in luxurious, stately homes staffed by servants. Surrounding the estate were fields, tended to by armies of agricultural laborers. Another part of the year was spent in London town houses, enjoying the political and social season. The town houses of the Georgian upper classes were substantial, often expensive buildings and grouped around London squares. Today, most have been divided up for use as hotels and expensive flats, but their grandeur remains. Members of this landed elite might also go to a spa for part of the year. Bath was particularly popular, as its great crescents of Georgian buildings testify.

The upper classes rode hard, drank heavily and fancied themselves the new Romans of the world, a concept fostered by their classical education. Restraint, discipline, proportion and moderation were the ideals of the ancient Greeks and Romans; many 18TH century Englishmen admired these ideals, but found it impossible to live up to them. The upper-class English of the Georgian era simply saw it as God's will that they should live in

Antony House in Cornwall, a great house built in the early 18ᵀᴴ century.

One of the glamorous women of the early 18TH century: Mrs. Graham portrayed by the famous artist, Thomas Gainsborough.

grand style and be placed over the millions of poor and toiling agricultural laborers who worked for a mere pittance.

The upper crust of 18TH century English society was extremely thin. Below them was a vital and growing middle class. Middle class numbers and importance had been rapidly growing since the late Middle Ages and would continue to do so in the next century as a result of the massive urbanization accompanying the Industrial Revolution. Then they would be strong enough to challenge the landed classes and question the legitimacy of aristocratic privilege and power. In the 18TH century they plied their trades and professions in all British cities and prospered without class conflict. The merchants among them became known as England's "shopocracy."

London had the greatest middle class concentration in the 18TH century. This was the London of that great figure of English literature, Dr. Johnson, who wrote that "He who tires of London tires of life." London's trade reached such proportions that it became the unchallenged leading commercial center of the world. Countless merchants, bankers, insurance agents and retailers—all clearly middle class types—enriched themselves and multiplied, as did teachers, doctors and lawyers.

Below the middle classes were the masses who often experienced cruelty, wretchedness and misery, whether they lived in urban or rural environments. In one way, 18TH century England was similar to Third World countries where the very rich and the very poor live in close proximity, but are worlds apart in terms of lifestyle. Debtors' prisons, infanticide, crime, an epidemic of alcoholism from cheap gin, widespread venereal disease, chronic malnutrition and all the illnesses it fostered—all of these things blighted the lives of the British poor during the Georgian era.

"Gin Lane," a famous engraving by William Hogarth showing the devastation from cheap gin. Only the pawn broker prospers.

Misery had always been the lot of the submerged masses of the world; but what made the 18TH century different was an incipient humanitarian movement that expressed a new social criticism and made efforts to provide remedies. Many hospitals and various charitable organizations originated in this century. Life was also ameliorated by increasing food supplies made available through new farming methods.

The most notable development in religion was Methodism. It was a branch of the established Anglican Church which Methodism's founder, John Wesley, found to be too cold, distant and impersonal for the needs of ordinary people. Wesley began to preach outdoors to the poor, stressing personal salvation. While he did not aim to break away from the Anglicans, a breach did result, and Protestantism gained a new denomination.

THE AMERICAN REVOLUTION FROM A BRITISH IMPERIAL PERSPECTIVE

Britain won all of its wars in the 18TH century, with the exception of the American Revolution. In each of these contests the main enemy remained Britain's historic foe, France, which was larger in terms of size, population and army. Britain nonetheless remained superior at sea and was able to get other nations to bear the brunt of dulling the onslaught of French armies bent upon expansion. In some wars Britain allied with Austria, and in others Prussia was the main continental collaborator. Since Britain was wealthy, allies were supported with cash and were expected to carry out most of the fighting on land in Europe. Britain sent armies of limited size to help out in continental campaigns. Eighteenth century warfare was not total; it was limited, disciplined and hedged with rules. After all, the officers respected the gentlemen gallantly fighting on the other side. The rank and file, however, were swept from the gutters of Europe, lured by food, clothing and a warm place to sleep when they were not putting their lives at risk.

These victories over the great autocratic and Catholic enemy, France, did much to develop British pride and nationalism, evident in two popular melodies of the time: "Rule Britannia" and "The British Grenadiers." Nevertheless, there was always an anti-war party in England that coexisted with a blustering, nationalistic pro-war party. The pro-war party consisted of Whigs and their allies who wanted to sweep the fleets of their enemies from the seas and take over other nations' colonies for the sake of trade profits. The anti-war party was supported by many Tories who paid taxes for the fleets and armies, but who did not directly profit from a greater British empire.

Victorious peace treaties usually rewarded Britain with parts of other empires. In India, the French were driven out and Britain's East India Company began to function as a colonial government. Robert Clive was an effective expansionist on behalf of the company who was able to organize Bengal as the base of British operations. In the Pacific, claims were laid to many future colonies by the explorations of Captain Cook, who was eventually slain by Hawaiian natives.

Americans are often confused by the wars of the 18TH century because a different set of names was used in the woods of North America, where the British and French and their respective Native American allies clashed throughout the century. The Seven Years' War, for instance, goes by the name of "The French and Indian War" in America.

As with most human conflicts, there are two points of view concerning the American Revolution: Americans are likely to inflate its historical importance, and the British are likely to see it as just another chapter of British imperial history. Indeed, American and British students are likely to come away with separate interpretations of the struggle.

Many events and principles of the American Revolution are familiar to most Americans, such as the Boston Tea Party, Paul Revere's Ride, Bunker Hill, Washington crossing the Delaware, the surrender of Cornwallis at Yorktown, the insistence upon "no taxation without representation," and the ideas of the Declaration of Independence. How, then, do the British view their only lost war?

When the bicentennial of the United States was being celebrated, the British put on a lavish display honoring the American Revolution. For them, as well as for Anglophile Americans, the American Revolution was really a civil war: there was a pro-revolutionary and an anti-revolutionary faction on each side of the Atlantic. Besides, Americans fought for traditional English freedoms that had been assured to Englishmen through their own heroic civil war struggles against the arbitrary rule of Charles I. After all, the cry of "no taxation without representation" was voiced against this king long before it was heard in America. For pro-revolutionaries, George III assumed the role of Charles I in the American Revolution, although historical hindsight reveals that a majority in a rather corrupt British Parliament was more responsible for handling the colonists in an authoritarian manner.

Famous Britons such as William Pitt the Elder, Edmund Burke and John Wilkes championed the colonists' struggles in the House of Commons, while in America at least a third of the population was what the British still choose to call "United Empire Loyalists." Americans have called them Tories. Estimates claim that another third in America was either neutral or would side with whichever force was in power locally; active revolutionaries were a minority—about a third of the population in America.

From a British point of view, Americans had been the beneficiaries of costly aid from the British navy and army since the 17TH century. The French along the St. Lawrence and their Indian allies had been a constant threat to the British colonies along the Atlantic coast. After half a dozen armed struggles, the French were finally driven from North America after the Seven Years' War in 1763. Thereafter, the American colonists could look forward to unhampered expansion westward.

For the British, the task of defending the Americans had been costly. American colonists did not pay a fair share towards their protection because they flaunted acts to regulate trade by smuggling. In addition, they did not provide sufficient men or money for the local militia that was supposed to help the British regular army.

To make the Americans pay their fair share of their defense, Parliament came up with the Stamp Act, which was already underway in Britain. A howl from the colonists led the British Parliament to abandon this scheme. The same situation resulted over the famous Townsend Duties. The British repealed all of them to suit the colonists, but retained the tax on tea to demonstrate Parliament's right to tax American colonists. As everyone knows, bales of privately owned tea came to float in Boston Harbor as a result of that celebrated episode of vandalism known as the Boston Tea Party. Military coercion followed in the

Boston area, providing the sparks that flared into revolution in 1775.

It took a year of fighting before independence was declared. This is because many sensible leaders on both sides of the Atlantic, including Benjamin Franklin, wanted to work out a compromise in the form of dominion status or Home Rule—the sort of arrangements that Canada, Australia and New Zealand were able to make without revolution later on. Yet the bloodshed of revolutions tends to escalate movement towards more radical solutions. Therefore, Americans chose independence after a year of fighting.

Despite the difficulties of bringing fleets and armies across the Atlantic, the British won a considerable number of battles and almost won the war. George Washington won few contests but spent most of his time in retreat. What really saved the American cause was the intervention of France and its allies, making the Revolution yet another world-wide war. French arms, well-trained French regular soldiers, and fleets under French command tipped the circumstances in North America in the colonists' favor.

It was fortunate for later relations between Britain and America that the Revolutionary War was not marred by the brutality and ferocity that have come to mark civil wars in the 20TH century. There were few atrocities against men in uniform or against civilians, with the leaders on both sides behaving like gentlemen. When the British were defeated in the American Revolution, the Tories were not lined up against walls and shot. In fact, defeated Tories could go to Canada, Bermuda, or back to Britain. Most relocated elsewhere in America, perhaps closer to the frontier, where they could cover up their former loyalty to Britain.

THE WORLD'S FIRST INDUSTRIAL REVOLUTION

The world's first Industrial Revolution came about in Britain, and all subsequent industrializations have adopted its pioneering techniques and methods to some extent. This makes the first Industrial Revolution an extremely important topic in world history, as well as in British history.

Britain's unprecedented leap into industrial production came from a spontaneous breakthrough. In actuality, several revolutions were going on simultaneously and they interacted with each other, thereby releasing concentrated economic energies that brought about amazing leaps in innovation. An agricultural revolution used new crops and techniques to raise food production, a necessary precondition for urban growth. A revolution in transportation quickened the flow of goods and services along improved roads, canals and, a few decades later, railroads. There was also a simultaneous revolution in technology which put specialized, powered machines in operation at much greater speed and efficiency. Last, there was a demographic revolution. In the 18TH century the death rate fell dramatically, and demographers still debate the complex subject of its causes. People married earlier, had more surviving children, and provided cheap labor for new industries as well as consumers for cheap, mass-produced goods.

Britain was in an advantageous position to utilize these simultaneous revolutionary changes. Britain had been favored by a preexisting extensive worldwide network of capitalistic trade, ample resources in coal and iron ore, a spirit of inventiveness, a skilled workforce in carpentry and metal trades, an elaborate financial infrastructure, good transportation facilities, an accumulation of capital to invest, and a government open to enterprise.

Loans and abundant low-wage labor enabled some entrepreneurs to experiment with machinery in order to meet massive demands for goods. Many of these new captains of industry rapidly went from debt to riches. Skilled workmen fashioned the new machines and maintained them, thus becoming the world's first modern engineers. Contraptions that worked in one industry inspired other entrepreneurs to apply them in other industries. The most effective new machines relied on the steam engine, developed earlier in Britain, in order to pump water out of coal mines. Both the steam engines and the coal mines they served would never have been developed had it not been for the shortage of wood in Britain. Over the centuries, an expanding population and expanding farm lands had drastically reduced the amount of wood available as fuel.

Cotton textile production became the pioneering industry for mass production, replacing hand-spinning first and then hand-weaving with mechanical production. There was a massive demand for cheap, machine-made cotton goods. Entrepreneurs made fortunes manufacturing cotton goods in Manchester and other northern cities. Uniquely, the raw material, cotton fibre, was imported from a great distance and brought to the factories using steam engines fueled by coal from nearby mines.

These interacting factors give some indication of the complexity of this spontaneous explosion of innovation in Britain that occurred between 1770 and 1840. During these years, the cumulative effect of so much new production enabled the economy to "take off and become airborne," an economist's phrase signifying permanent, self-sustaining growth and development. Changes came fast—often massive, irreversible, and dramatic—as when the world's first railway grid was constructed. Much of the labor changed from hand to machine; most goods came to be produced in large factories rather than in small shops; more and more consumer goods were produced at generally decreasing cost per item; and fortunes were made quickly, often by mass-producing ordinary household goods.

All of this had a profound effect on the structure of British society. Industrialization led to rapid urban growth, the creation of an urban factory proletariat, and a broadening of the middle class strata. Rapidly growing towns and cities were soon in need of more lawyers, doctors, teachers, bankers and managers. Eventually, Britain had the world's first society with an urban majority where the middle classes were so numerous and influential that they came to play a dominant role in important aspects of politics and culture. This was a key feature underlying the society of the 19TH century.

For the generations undergoing these changes for the first time, the costs in human suffering were staggering, as any reader of Dickens or Marx knows. Overcrowding, periodic unemployment, low wages, poor sanitation and wretched working conditions were all prevalent in the worst stages of the Industrial Revolution. But once industrial production was underway, widespread prosperity and comfort benefited most. Britain became the first place in the world where the majority of the population came to enjoy what we have come to call the "affluent" society. Since then, most of Europe, America and Japan have followed Britain's model and have become modern, industrially developed areas.

Britain still celebrates its special role in the Industrial Revolution. Museums display old machinery as treasures; huge railway museums have been erected; and places in the industrial

Bradford's factories. Modern eyes see the pollution and ugliness, but to most Victorians the scene signified jobs and prosperity.

northern part of England have been set aside to commemorate the origin of the factory system.

There is also a psychological inheritance from this era. For roughly a century, Britain led the world in technology. British goods were produced more efficiently and with a higher level of engineering than anywhere else in the world. By contrast, American industrial development in the 19TH century was in its early stages in the North, at least until the stimulation of the American Civil War. In general, America was a vast agrarian area noted for producing raw materials and foodstuffs. American food, cotton and timber were regularly exchanged for enticing, cheap goods from Britain's booming factories.

Today, when Japan, Germany and the United States lead Britain in most, but not all, "high tech" and "post-industrial" advances, Britons remember their long span of superiority in the 19TH century with a mixture of remorse and pride.

THE IMPACT OF THE FRENCH REVOLUTION AND THE NAPOLEONIC ERA: 1789-1815

As the storm of the French Revolution gathered strength, most English people were pleased. It wasn't just that their main international rival was weakened by internal turmoil; what gratified the English was how the French seemed to be imitating them. The French called an old, dormant legislative body into life and passed measures that curtailed royal powers. It seemed that French autocracy was going to be replaced by an English-style limited, constitutional monarchy.

Enthusiasm for the French Revolution soon cooled and was replaced by horror as the French took increasingly radical steps. The violence of the Parisian mobs, the executions of the guillotine, the destruction of the ranks of society, the confiscation of church and noble property—all these appalled the English observers. They even found the execution of the monarch unsettling, though it had been done in England over a century before. Only a handful of radicals continued to be enthusiastic about the French proclamation of liberty, equality and fraternity, careers open to talent and not birth, and freedom from kings and priests in the name of reason. For the rest of the population, it seemed that Britain's class structure, property, religion and way of life were menaced by the French Revolution.

Soon it became clear that instead of weakening France, the Revolution was actually strengthening Britain's historic enemy by releasing a powerful social energy. French armies poured across Europe, larger than ever and inspired by revolutionary zeal. A successful young general, Napoleon Bonaparte, emerged to bring order and stability to the Revolution in France and to spread its benefits to the rest of Europe by conquest. To the English, Napoleon was the modernized, autocratic replacement of the French monarchs and much more dangerous. Before long, England was locked in a perilous set of wars aimed at defeating Napoleon.

The years of the French Revolution and Napoleon's victories were exciting and heroic for the English as great monuments all over Britain confirm. For a time, Britain faced invasion alone, a situation that was repeated again in 1940 when the Nazis threatened the island.

Two great heroes emerged to stop the French. Horatio Nelson, one-armed, one-eyed and just over five-feet tall, defeated a large French-led fleet at Trafalgar in 1805. He died at the battle's close, and today his statue is a landmark of London, towering above Trafalgar Square. The other hero was the Duke of Wellington, who stopped Napoleon's army at the famous and very close Battle of Waterloo in 1815. Wellington continued to offer sage advice to British rulers until the middle of the 19TH century.

Times of tension and change can often bring on a burst of cultural creativity. In this era great romantic poets and writers flourished: Keats, Shelley, Wordsworth, Coleridge and Sir Walter Scott. Romanticism emphasized the overwhelming forces of nature, religion and emotion. It celebrated the glories of the Middle Ages and distant, exotic cultures. Romanticism left its impress upon architecture, art, music and literature, as classical restraints and proportions were surmounted by newfound surges of feeling.

Not surprisingly, a British intellectual revolution coincided with the upheavals of the French and Industrial revolutions. Remarkably, it had a dual nature. Some famous intellectuals stressed the need to apply human reason exclusively, while others emphasized reliance upon spirit and emotions to explain the dramatic new worlds unfolding before them.

Among the rationalists were Jeremy Bentham and Parson Thomas Malthus. Bentham regarded the law as a great hodge-podge from the past that needed rational reconstruction on the principle of promoting the greatest happiness for the greatest number. Malthus frightened contemporaries with his theory of excessive population growth; he hypothesized that the population increases geometrically, that is, 1, 2, 4, 8, 16 and so on, while food supply only increases arithmetically, 1, 2, 3, 4 and so on.

The most influential person among those championing spirit and emotions was undoubtedly John Wesley, founder of the Methodist denomination. Methodism encouraged political conservatism, teaching people to accept their lot and to hope for equality in the next world. The middle class was attracted to Methodism's disciplined values of duty, thrift and work. How important Methodism was to the working class is debatable. Employers certainly encouraged the spread of this denomination among their employees in an effort to prevent radical, revolutionary ideas and to promote highly productive virtues. As a result, a long tradition of working-class leaders with Methodist backgrounds began.

Methodism was but one part of a wider movement called Evangelicalism, whose overall purpose was to revitalize Christianity. One branch of the established Anglican Church became evangelical. They practiced good works and launched moral crusades in a grave, earnest, and humorless manner. Their most famous achievement was the abolition of the slave trade (1807) and slavery in the British Empire (1833).

THE EARLY 19ᵀᴴ CENTURY: THE ERA OF THE REFORM BILL

The Regency era began in 1811, the year that future King George IV came to rule as Prince Regent in place of George III, who had become mentally incapacitated or, as he was described, "sad and mad." In style and outlook, the Regency era is said to have continued until his death in 1830.

In art and architecture, the Regency style was powerful. Buildings tended to be massive and neoclassical, which meant the imposition of regularity, order and discipline. Greek and Roman motifs prevailed, such as *bas reliefs* and Doric columns. Many great structures in London date from this era, especially along Regent's Street and in the areas around Trafalgar Square and Regent's Park.

For Continental Europe, the early 19TH century was a revolutionary era, as impulses toward equality from the French Revolution convulsed Europe in waves of upheavals occurring in 1820, 1830 and 1848. Britain was unique in avoiding revolution. Why was this so? How were the British able to transform their ancient political institutions to accommodate the needs and demands of that ever-growing urban and industrial sector without violence and destruction? The answer is complex. A key factor was that the deeply-rooted and somewhat representative Parliamentary system was able to reform itself through a set of gradual compromises. This satisfied enough people for the time being, thereby thwarting the drive for change through violent revolution.

The British Parliament passed a number of Reform Bills in the 19TH century—in 1832, 1867 and 1884—each of which broadened the franchise to give more males the opportunity to vote. The first was the greatest because it led to the gradual achievement of democracy. The Reform Bill of 1832 gave the vote to those in the middle class by creating a uniform franchise based upon property. Also, new electoral districts were created for the new industrial towns which had been underrepresented in the old House of Commons. New seats were created while the small and corrupt electoral districts, called "rotten" or "pocket" boroughs, were eliminated. Such boroughs were sprinkled throughout most of the south of England; they had been the strongholds of the landed classes and the basis of much of their political power in Parliament.

The Reform Bill of 1832 marked both the successful inclusion of the most prosperous components of the new industrial society into the political process, and the diminution of the power of the landed classes. It also indicated that evolution and gradualism, not revolution, were to be the hallmarks of change for the British constitution. In contrast, on the continent of Europe, middle class types were apt to be ardent revolutionaries, at least until the middle of the century. In Britain the middle class came to believe that their limited, constitutional monarchy was moving towards greater liberalism. They appreciated their government's drive towards freer markets and a growth of their own personal wealth under a limited monarchy. Hence, they supported and protected the system against any would-be revolutionaries. Therefore, the Reform Bill of 1832 guaranteed that 1688 would be the last year of revolution in British history.

The bill did not go far enough for the British working classes, who had agitated for democracy. Until 1848, British workers had been attracted by French revolutionary slogans for democracy and equality. Discontented workers formed an organization called the Chartist Movement, backing the People's Charter, which demanded universal male voting rights supported by such democratic safeguards as payment of members and equal electoral districts.

When the Continent flared in violent revolution in 1848, all that British workers accomplished was to march to Parliament unarmed and present a petition for the People's Charter; a few windows were broken, but these were minor incidents. The government had mustered a great force to ensure that there would not be a violent outbreak. Police and newly recruited "special constables," most of them volunteers from the newly-enfranchised middle class, ringed the Chartist procession. Backing them up were carefully hidden regular troops led by the Duke of Wellington, the now ancient hero of Waterloo. The government did not take chances when it came to the remote possibility of a revolution flaring in England.

Economic conditions in the early 19TH century made the Chartists militant reformers. Boom and bust prevailed in the economy. When the factories throve the workers fared well, and when the factories closed the workers were plunged into misery. Conditions improved considerably after 1850, but until mid-century it was common to speak of two Englands: the England of the rich and the England of the poor. Some of the most distressing scenes from Dickens' novels can be attributed to these miserable times for workers.

THE MAGNIFICENCE OF THE VICTORIAN ERA: 1837-1901

The long and relatively peaceful 64-year reign of Queen Victoria left an indelible stamp on the England of today, both materially and psychologically. It was the time of Britain's apogee, or high point, when the nation led the world in science, technology, politics, and power. Never before and never since the Victorian era has Britain been so influential on the world stage. Britain's role in the 19TH century can be compared to that of the United States in much of the 20TH century, except that Britain did not face a decades-long international rivalry as America had with the former Soviet Union. *Pax Britannica*, or the peace of Britain, was imposed and welcomed on all oceans and many

Victorian poverty and overcrowding depicted by Gustave Dore.

neighboring lands. Britain's vast and unchallenged navy served as the nation's instrument of supremacy.

Progress was the all-important word for the Victorian era. Victorians believed in it fervently and saw themselves as the most progressive people in the world. This conviction was constantly reaffirmed by continual inventions and scientific advances on a broad front, thereby gaining ever more control over nature for the apparent benefit of humankind. Victorians measured progress in many tangible ways, for example, in dramatically increased production of coal, iron, textiles, shipbuilding and consumer goods. The world's first railway system transformed the landscape, and everywhere efficiency and speed came to be considered British hallmarks. Most Victorians were pious Christians who saw these advances as indications that they were God's new chosen people, destined to prosper and discover God's handiwork.

Victorians also measured progress in politics. Old bastions of hereditary privilege and discrimination were removed one by one in a free Parliament where reason, discussion, debate and voting determined decisions. Literacy and education advanced with a simultaneous increase in voter population.

Victorians were free from many worries of the 20TH century. Pollution was not as serious a concern as it is today, and science did not appear as a dangerous genie. Modern totalitarianism, either fascism or communism, had not yet emerged from the rubble of war and despair on the Continent. It was a time when Britain's upper and middle-class subjects had the most envied and admired lifestyles. The whole world seemed to want to develop along British lines. Limited, constitutional representative government became the ideal goal for reformers and revolutionaries in less fortunate countries worldwide.

The Victorians exhibited psychological characteristics that directly influenced 19TH and early 20TH century Americans. Ideally, Victorians were moral, pious and committed to the work ethic. Thrift, discipline, honesty, temperance, hard work, earnestness, obedience to God's Word, and cleanliness were all solid Victorian virtues. All sexual expression was to be confined to marriage and repressed otherwise. While contemporary lifestyles for most English and American people have departed from Victorian virtues, it can be argued that the Victorian psychological inheritance is still active, contributing to feelings of guilt, the penchant for cleanliness, and the phenomenon of the workaholic.

SOME VICTORIAN ACHIEVEMENTS

Famous Victorians are legion. This was the world of Charles Dickens, Rudyard Kipling, Thomas Hardy, Sir Walter Scott and Alfred, Lord Tennyson, to name but a few literary greats. It was the world of Gilbert and Sullivan on stage. In politics, two great figures dominated the later years of Victoria's reign: Benjamin Disraeli, a novelist of Jewish background, and William Gladstone, the embodiment of open-minded liberalism and pious leadership. In foreign policy, the irascible and dashing Lord Palmerston celebrated and fostered British interests throughout the world with a headline-grabbing flair that appealed to British pride and nationalism.

What about the Queen who gave her name to this era? She was small, proud, dutiful, earnest and a hard-working monarch. She displayed all of the virtues of her most progressive subjects, particularly those from the newly-enfranchised middle class. To them, Victoria's behavior must have been a great relief

110

after the numerous scandals associated with her Hanoverian relatives.

Leading statesmen instructed her on how to be a strictly constitutional monarch. She was to reign and not to rule. This meant that she was to be informed by her ministers about government policy and she could respond to them with her advice and views, none of which had to be acted upon. She was to accede to her cabinet's appointments, bills, and wishes automatically.

Victoria's adult life can be divided into two periods: the time when she was married and her long period of widowhood. Her beloved husband was Prince Consort Albert, a German like nearly all of Victoria's ancestors. Albert assumed the role of a constitutional consort, but Victoria, as a proper wife of the era, submitted to the firm will of her husband. When he died suddenly of typhus in middle age, Victoria went into a deep and morbid mourning. When she recovered later in life, she had become the revered symbol of the greatest empire that the world had ever seen.

In Victoria's heyday, the British Empire expanded in all directions, stretching over "palm and pine." "The sun never sets on the British Empire" was a cliché in Victorian times, meaning that the sun had to be shining on some part of it somewhere on the globe during all twenty-four hours. Eventually, one-fourth of the earth's surface and its people came to live under some kind of British authority—a remarkable achievement for such a small island. There was an informal empire of trade, wherein British goods, ships, money and services operated profitably almost everywhere.

Britain was unchallenged at sea and could send gunboats to defend the rights of British subjects anywhere in the world. For

This cartoon shows Benjamin Disraeli seeking to make Victoria Empress of India.

William Gladstone, the great Liberal prime minister, at age 75.

A statue of Queen Victoria in Asia, just one of many statues of her that were erected in every part of the British Empire.

most of the era foreign policy consisted of "splendid isolation," meaning that there were no entangling alliances with any important states. Victoria's army was involved in a number of small but glorious wars against natives in the far reaches of the empire. Each of these wars resulted in many medals and promotions. Rare British defeats, such as those against the Zulus at Isandhlwana in 1879 or the Dervishes of the Sudan in 1885, were vigorously avenged in devastating campaigns. Britain was involved in only one major European war in the period from 1815 to 1914: the grim and inconclusive Crimean War, fought with the French, Turks and Italians against the Russians from 1854 to 1856. Two examples of heroism remembered from this dismal struggle were the charge of the Light Brigade and the hospital work of Florence Nightingale, the founder of the modern nursing profession.

The Victorians were great builders, inventors, developers and producers—pioneers in harnessing machines to their economy. Goods of all sorts from the Victorian era can be found in Britain today as well as in many other parts of the world. Much of their furniture and mass-produced items are considered to be valuable antiques today. In addition, great Victorian buildings, bridges and aqueducts, and railway system testify to the energy of these people.

It may be argued that younger people today tend to appreciate the "charm" of Victoriana more than the many older people who grew up with it in their parents' or grandparents' homes. Inside the home, furniture was typically overstuffed and rooms were cluttered with fancy knick-knacks. The exteriors of homes and buildings commonly employed an ornate "gingerbread"-style decoration. All types of structures, even functional railway bridges, received Victorian superfluous decoration.

Contingents from all over the British Empire brought to London to celebrate Victoria's jubilee.

Much of the Victorians' architecture is eclectic, borrowed from classical Renaissance and medieval styles. However, one exception is the beautiful and unique Crystal Palace made of glass and steel girders—a Victorian structure that foreshadowed the great skyline buildings of the 20TH century. It housed the first world's fair, featuring displays of British industrial machinery among many other exhibits. Glass and steel were also used impressively in Victorian railway stations. Another Victorian innovation was the development of suspension bridges, which were small compared with the giant 20TH century American examples of this kind of span.

Overall, the Middle Ages provided the favorite source of the Victorians' artistic inspiration and thereby reveals their essential romanticism. Medieval castles, cathedrals and knights in shining armor were widely celebrated in literature and art. Victorian appreciation for the Middle Ages has often confused contemporary foreign visitors. Many seemingly medieval creations turn out to be just over one hundred years old. Visitors may go into a grim, turreted hulk of an Anglican church in suburban London and think it to be the very essence of a medieval edifice, until discovering that the Victorians erected it in the 1880s.

SOME VICTORIAN PARADOXES

Dynamic and complex Victorian society gave rise to several striking but true paradoxes. To Marx it was paradoxical that the world's most advanced industrial state had a bourgeois working class and a bourgeois upper class. (Bourgeois is a word for the middle class, generally favored by continental Europeans.)

117

A unique Victorian building: The Crystal Palace, where the first world's fair was held.

A painting by John Martin depicting the romantic elements of medievalism, the dedicated musician and overwhelming nature.

Indeed, the triumph of middle-class values, attested to by the splendid performance of the new economy, set standards for the other classes as well, at least outwardly.

Another Victorian paradox involved the celebration of the market economy at the same time that the first modern state intervention in the economy made considerable headway. *Laissez-faire* was a policy that urged the state to allow the economic process to proceed unhindered by intervention. Victorian ministers did indeed remove many tariff barriers and old guild regulations. Middle-class liberals throughout the world cheered them on, believing that unregulated capitalism would become the greatest source of riches for everyone.

Victorian ministers gave lip service to *laissez-faire* principles at the same time that they were busy promoting considerable state intervention along modern lines. The first stage of this procedure would be to gather facts and statistics and place them in an official report. Second, Parliamentary leaders would study the reports and design legislation. Third, the proposed new legislation would be debated in Parliament and settled by a majority vote. Fourth, a governmental bureaucracy would be established to apply the new legislation. These procedures were followed to create hundreds of laws designed to accommodate the new economy to society's needs. Good examples are laws regulating the hours and working conditions for factory workers, laws preventing the exploitation of children, laws achieving a sanitary water supply, and laws regulating trade unions. Paradoxically, then, the origins of the modern welfare state can be traced to the growth of a Victorian bureaucracy in the heyday of *laissez-faire*.

Another Victorian paradox involves sexuality. The Victorian middle-class ideal was that all sex be confined to married couples.

Ideally, married middle-class women were not supposed to work outside of the home. They were to concentrate instead on raising children and making the home as perfect as possible for their hard-working husbands. Actually, affluent Victorian women had servants and therefore considerable time to read novels and work on their elaborate dress and hairstyles. These women were to be decorative and amusing, and their strength was to rest in their moral rectitude and spirituality. Men, on the other hand, were supposed to fall short of women spiritually and emotionally, but they were regarded as far superior to women in mental and physical strength and ability.

Victorians applied a double standard to sexuality. When a man transgressed by becoming involved in sex outside of marriage, it was attributed to the powerful urges of his "animal nature." Respectable women, however, were not supposed to have such inclinations. Certainly, Victorian men dreaded the thought of being cuckolds responsible for someone else's child. Therefore, unfaithful men were treated much less harshly than their female counterparts. Wives discovered cheating were usually thrown out of their homes. Victorian divorce laws were very expensive to apply and heavily weighted in favor of men. Unmarried daughters who came home pregnant were often expelled by their dominant Victorian fathers.

What is most paradoxical about Victorian sexuality is its hypocrisy which, for Victorians, was the compliment that vice paid to virtue. Proper Victorian husbands were expected to be faithful. Yet Victorian England swarmed with prostitutes. London, in particular, had numerous brothels, some catering to the most extraordinary fetishes.

Still another Victorian paradox was the sense of romanticism amidst intense material preoccupations. Most Victorians were obsessed with making things and making money. The world of business was a harsh world of facts, figures and balances. Yet, at the same time, Victorian paintings celebrate sentimental dogs and children, medieval heroes and imaginative fairies. Authors, many of whom are still avidly read today, employed comparable themes. The romanticism of Victorian art and literature seems to have functioned as an escape or a change of pace from the harsh, practical and prosaic realities Victorians faced.

Many contemporary English and Americans still curl up with a Sherlock Homes mystery or a Dickens novel and transport themselves back to foggy nights in Victorian London. Although the fogs may no longer be there, thanks to strict air ordinances, rich deposits of Victoriana are still to be found everywhere in England. Contemporary America might have something of its own version of the Victorian paradox of romantic escapism: The nation that builds interstate highways, computers, cars and aircraft carriers is also responsible for the romantic worlds of Walt Disney and Star Wars.

THE EDWARDIAN ERA: 1901-1914

Although the king for whom the era is named died in 1910, the Edwardian era is generally regarded as the period from 1901, the year Victoria died, to 1914, the year that World War I erupted. Impressions of the quality of life in Britain during this time span vary considerably. The wealthy and well-born usually remember the Edwardian era as a glorious sunset when empire, capitalism, social life and British influence throughout the world were splendid. Alternately, the humbly-born might recall

Victorian sentimentalism is shown in "No Walk Today," by Sophie Anderson.

the huge disparities between rich and poor, the long hours of work for low pay, the slums, and the lack of all but the beginnings of welfare provisions. Yet all might agree that it was a brassier, more strident age than the Victorian era. The popular song of the times, "Ta-Ra-Ra-Boom-De-Ay," captures something of its essence.

Several simultaneous breakthroughs in technology have prompted some to declare that a second industrial revolution occurred during these years. The internal combustion engine was developed and applied to cars and airplanes. The telephone, gramophone, telegraph and motion picture were other influential innovations of the Edwardian era.

The Edwardian era began at the conclusion of an imperialistic war in South Africa, the Boer War, which the British won at considerable cost. Cecil Rhodes, a diamond and gold magnate, was suspected of operating behind the scenes to bring down two small Afrikaner republics. The Afrikaners, Dutch descendants who had lived in South Africa since the 17TH century, had the sympathy of the Europeans because they appeared to be underdogs heroically resisting aggressive British imperialism. The British made matters worse by terminating Afrikaner guerrilla resistance by means of a scorched earth policy and the use of concentration camps.

The war revealed the widespread unpopularity of the British in Europe. British recognition of their isolation and a sense of the hostility directed against them led to attempts to engage in *ententes*, or loose alliances, with European powers thereafter. This in turn helped to bring Britain into World War I.

No matter how high the status of British capitalism, the Edwardian era also marked the beginning of important aspects of the modern welfare state. Pensions and national health insurance were inaugurated during this time. While Britain lagged behind Germany and other European states in this regard, it was far ahead of the United States in making such provisions.

Socialist theory also made headway in the Edwardian period. One characteristically British kind of socialism to emerge was that of the Fabian Socialists, whose membership included George Bernard Shaw and Sidney and Beatrice Webb. The former was the greatest English playwright since Shakespeare, and the latter were a team of important social scientists. The Fabian Socialists were intellectuals who sought to convince influential people of the rational and just nature of socialism brought about by democratic means. At first they worked to prove the practical nature of socialism at the local level by taking over such things as gas and water services, which gave them the nickname of "gas and water socialists."

About the same time, masses of unskilled workers enrolled in large, militant unions. These unions and several groups of socialists came together in the Edwardian era to form the Labour Party. While it was only a minor party in the period before World War I, its influence and the inspiration of the Fabians would come to the fore later, particularly after World War II. In all of this, Marxists played a very small role. In general, British Labour politics did not accept the Marxist view of the inevitability of class warfare.

Another movement of the Edwardian era that was to have a major bearing upon the future was the Suffragette movement, which was aimed at gaining votes for women. The right to vote was viewed as the key to ending male dominance and discrimination in many fields. After peaceful demonstrations had been regularly ignored, the more militant suffragettes deliberately broke the law by highly visible and outrageous means. They set

The "Black Ascot" of 1910, when the fashionable horse race was attended by people in mourning to honor the death of Edward VII.

fires, chained themselves in public places, and destroyed private property in order to draw attention to their movement and its unmet goals. When imprisoned, they went on hunger strikes and the authorities responded by subjecting them to the unpleasant process of forced-feeding.

Another source of tension was Ireland, where Home Rule was destined to occur. Home Rule was called "dominion status" elsewhere, an arrangement that would allow the Irish to run their own domestic affairs the way Canadians or Australians did by that time.

The key to the Home Rule struggle was a major Act that had passed Parliament in 1911, severely limiting the power of the House of Lords. Henceforth this ancient body could only delay legislation for a limited period of time and could not block it the way the United States Senate can block legislation passed in the House of Representatives. It made Britain's government virtually unicameral, or one-chambered. For Ireland, this meant that self-rule would be passed. Previously, the House of Lords had always blocked Home Rule legislation.

Nevertheless, in Ulster, militant Protestants resisted the sovereign rule of the British Parliament by declaring that they would rather fight than be dominated by a Roman Catholic majority ruling from Dublin. Then, as now, the British were faced with a seemingly insoluble Irish situation. Civil war loomed in Ireland and was only prevented by the outbreak of World War I. Home Rule was delayed for the duration of the war so that Protestant and Catholic energies could pour into the war effort. The militant suffragettes and the contentious union members also focused on the war effort. World War I absorbed whole currents of tension and potential violence stemming from Edwardian times into its own great vortex of conflict.

For the rich who were not interested in women's rights, socialism, poverty or Ireland, the Edwardian era was delightful. The monarch, Edward VII, personified many of the tastes of the wealthy in his time. Queen Victoria's eldest son had always been something of a hedonist and Francophile, at odds with his strict Germanophile upbringing. Edward and much of upper-class society indulged themselves in wine, women, song and spectacular consumption in a style that parallels the Gilded Age in America when American millionaires reveled in garish materialism. In a way, this supremely confident Edwardian society suffered the same fate as their greatest nautical achievement, the Titanic. This great ship, declared to be "unsinkable," hit an iceberg and went down in 1912. The iceberg, for British society, was the onset of the horror of four years of brutal war.

THE ERA OF WORLD WAR I

The joys of Edwardian Britain came to an abrupt end with the outbreak of World War I in the summer of 1914. The United States entered the war late, in 1917, and most of the American forces never reached the front lines. While America suffered over 50,000 deaths, Britain suffered 750,000 deaths. In fact, Britain lost twice as many of its people in World War I than in World War II. This is a startling statistic, considering that the Second World War was a longer contest, taking place from 1939 to 1945 and bringing tens of thousands of British civilian deaths from heavy air bombing.

In addition to those who were killed or wounded during World War I, as well as those who lost husbands, fathers, sons, brothers, sweethearts and potential mates, the war brought psychological ramifications that were strong and complex. Such phenomena as alienation from Western civilization and disgust at formerly esteemed nationalism and patriotism surfaced in many veterans. On the Continent, the war led to a new kind of violent nationalism called fascism.

The war also brought a high concentration of collectivization, or state control, of the economy. Although this was disestablished after the war, it was reapplied later in the century. The war demonstrated what the state could do in allocating raw materials, taking over production, and regulating everything from finance to the workforce. It also demonstrated what women could do. For the first time, women were welcomed in the factories and on the farms to do work traditionally assigned to men. Yet, when the war was over, they were expected to step aside and go back to being wives and mothers.

In Britain, it is not uncommon to hear people call World War I "the First German War," and indeed many still blame the war upon the Kaiser and German militarism. Yet historians have shown that all of the major participants and some of the minor ones were to a degree guilty and innocent regarding the outbreak of the war. Seen from this perspective, the ruthless sacrifice of the blood and treasure of European civilization from 1914 to 1918 was simply a tragedy on a monumental scale.

When the Archduke Franz Ferdinand of Austria-Hungary was assassinated by a Serbian nationalist or terrorist in the streets of Sarajevo in Bosnia Herzegovina, a diplomatic crisis ensued. To British people, the situation seemed to be just one more crisis in a long series of Balkan troubles. Unfortunately, this Balkan crisis got out of hand and escalated into a small war between Austria and Serbia. This in turn escalated into a world war as the major powers lined up to support their allies.

Britain had an *entente* with France and Russia, two nations with whom Britain was able to smooth out imperial rivalries. Anglo-German amity had been ruined in the Edwardian era by the headlong effort of the Germans to build a great fleet. The German fleet was a direct threat to Britain because the island nation had to import a substantial amount of its food and raw materials from overseas. What helped the number of British politicians who wavered to decide to go to war in 1914 was the German invasion of Belgium, a country whose neutrality was guaranteed by Britain and several other powers. Belgium had a particular strategic significance because it was the logical place from which to launch an invasion of the British Isles.

British participation in World War I was similar to that of France and Germany in that it involved costly campaigns that seemed to go nowhere. The Western Front consisted of a maze of trenches stretching from Switzerland's border across France and Belgium to the sea. The British fought on the western portion of the Western Front, mostly in the flat portion of Belgium. The most tragic losses "in Flanders' fields" came along the Somme River. Up to 60,000 British casualties were recorded there in a single day of fighting. Year after year, armies on both sides hurled masses of foot soldiers against barbed wire, machine guns and artillery without breaking the stalemate. Defensive weapons clearly had the advantage. The offensive weapons of the next war—the airplane and the tank—were in early experimental stages during World War I.

Gallipoli was an ill-fated campaign that sought to open a way through to Russia via the Turkish Dardanelles, the waterway between the Mediterranean Sea, controlled by the Allies, and the Black Sea, controlled by Russia. Winston

British troops leaving the trenches for one of many costly attacks during World War I.

Churchill, at the Admiralty, was unfairly blamed for the costly British failure at Gallipoli.

At sea, there was only one major surface battle, Jutland, which was something of a draw. The much-feared German fleet stayed in port thereafter. The submarine fleet kept active, however, threatening to cut off vital supplies. Convoy tactics eventually turned the tide against the submarines.

The great British leader of World War I was David Lloyd George, a Welshman who rose from obscurity to become a leading Liberal minister in the Edwardian era. When the war began, he displayed his ability by meeting the challenge of a munitions shortage. Then he engineered the overthrow of the less able prime minister so that he could take the office himself. David Lloyd George was a dynamo of a leader and a magnificent orator. In many ways he played the role in World War I that Winston Churchill would come to play in World War II. He certainly had the will to victory. Yet he had a negative side as well, facing not unfounded accusations of corruption, ruthlessness and guile as well as public resentment of his domineering style. He remains a controversial figure to this day and is best-loved in his native Wales.

Britain did win a few clear victories on the periphery of the main effort of the war. Palestine was wrested away from the Ottoman Turks, and the Germans were defeated in Africa. But the war was finally decided by attrition on the Western Front. Russia dropped out of the war the same year that the United States entered it, putting the whole focus on fighting in France. After coming close to winning in a last surge in 1918, the Germans called for an armistice which ended the war. Shortly thereafter the harsh Peace of Versailles was imposed upon the Germans—a peace that became one of the causes of the next world war.

THE INTERWAR ERA: 1918-1939

After the ferocious destruction of World War I, the English tried to return to normalcy. But the Edwardian assurance and opulence did not return for Britain in general. The interwar era can be described as gray, grim and depressed. Unemployment was high throughout nearly the whole era, with some families living on the "dole," or welfare payments, decade after decade. Britain's most notable but aged industries—shipbuilding, coal mining, steel and textiles—were hardest hit by chronic depression. Meanwhile, new light industries, such as the manufacture of electrical appliances, developed considerably, providing British consumers with all sorts of new products including tinned (canned) goods and various synthetics. On the one hand, there was material progress for many consumers, but on the other there was bare subsistence for the unemployed millions. Hunger marches, strikes and lockouts signified the rancor of the times. An attempted general strike, aimed at bringing out the workers of key industries and thereby paralyzing the state, failed ingloriously in 1926. One way to appreciate the more dismal aspects of the period is to read George Orwell's *The Road to Wigan Pier*.

The dominant political figure of the period was Stanley Baldwin, a stolid, business-like, and rather dull Conservative. Often the 1920s and early 1930s are called the "age of Baldwin." Labour mustered its first brief governments in the interwar period as well. These were governments formed in coalition. Labour never had a clear-cut majority until after World War II. The first Labour prime minister was J. Ramsay McDonald, who is still disparaged by many Labourites today for having sold out to the establishment once he got into power. His defenders point to his need to compromise in the particular circumstances he faced.

The interwar period marked the beginning of the dissolution of the British Empire. Ireland was the first to go. A small but violent rebellion had occurred in 1916. The British overreacted to this "Easter Rebellion" by executing many of its leaders, who became martyrs and thereby made the movement for Irish independence much stronger. Home Rule would no longer be enough for the increasing number of those sympathetic to the rebellion. An independent republic was now desired by Irishmen willing to fight a civil war to attain it. Britain sought to repress them, sending in the hated "Black and Tans," a voluntary and mercenary paramilitary force. Eventually, Lloyd George signed a peace treaty in 1922 which granted sovereignty to all of Ireland except six counties in the province of Ulster.

Royalty became the focus of romantic drama. George V died in 1936, after reigning for twenty-six years as a dutiful and appreciated monarch. His eldest son succeeded him as Edward VIII. However, he only lasted for less than a year because of a dramatic set of events that captured headlines: He had fallen hopelessly in love with Wallis Simpson, a twice-divorced American. Given the standards of the time, their liaison and his plan to marry her were scandalous. Consequently, the king of England abdicated his throne so that he could, in his words, marry the woman he loved. Thereafter he became an exile, with the title Duke of Windsor, and Mrs. Simpson became his duchess. Together they dedicated their lives to frivolous social affairs in various elegant places abroad. Edward's brother reigned in his place from 1936 to 1952 as George VI. He was the father of Queen Elizabeth II.

Britain had its equivalent of America's "roaring twenties," complete with flappers and jazz; but the dominant notes of life in interwar Britain for too many people were those of depression. With bitter memories of difficult post-World War I years still vivid, the English were very willing to go along with the Labour Party's proposals for a new kind of state after the next war reached its conclusion.

APPEASEMENT: 1934-1939

The shadow of World War I loomed over foreign policy during the interwar period. Britain and other nations made numerous attempts to achieve disarmament or at least to prevent arms races. These efforts proved futile when the rise of fascist dictatorships in Germany, Italy and several lesser countries produced regimes committed to extreme nationalism and militarism. Only armed force could block their chronic, endemic aggression, but before this lesson could be learned, Britain had already endured grave humiliations in foreign policy.

Prime Minister Neville Chamberlain, always impeccably dressed, conveyed the impression of a most reasonable and sensible British gentleman. Since the Treaty of Versailles was more discredited with each passing year, Chamberlain believed that he could appease the grievances of Nazi Germany by making sensible, reasonable and timely concessions. This policy of appeasement reached its greatest intensity when the national sovereignty of Czechoslovakia was virtually surrendered to a bullying Hitler at Munich in 1938.

When Nazi aggression continued, Chamberlain and his followers realized that appeasement had been a futile policy for

The famous photo of Neville Chamberlain returning from the Munich conference in 1938, waving a signed agreement with Hitler, which he said brought "peace in our time."

dealing with fascist dictators. Thereafter the British government began to rearm as fast as possible, while British diplomacy changed course and confronted aggression by announcing agreements to go to war if certain other small states were violated. Therefore, Britain went to war in September 1939, when Germany attacked Poland.

The word "appeasement" passed into English usage as a pejorative term, meaning "to give in to aggression." Its original meaning had been much more neutral, betokening attempts at conciliation. One outstanding British politician, Winston Churchill, had warned against appeasement all along. Consequential events proved him right, and when the war against Germany floundered in 1939 and 1940, Churchill became prime minister at the age of sixty-five—an age when most men either look forward to retirement or are already retired.

BRITAIN IN WORLD WAR II: 1939-1945

After the Japanese attack on Pearl Harbor on December 7, 1941, brought the United States into the war, a flood of men and materials from North America poured into Britain and crossed the English Channel in the D-Day invasion of June 1944. Both in Europe and the Pacific, the United States was clearly the dominant partner in the Anglo-American alliance.

Interesting cultural exchanges took place between the millions of Americans in uniform and their British hosts. Many marriages resulted, and there was also some generally friendly rivalry. Americans complained about such things as the beer being warm. One Briton, exasperated at the deluge of Americans, made the famous declaration that American troops were "overpaid, oversexed and over here." The famous American riposte was that Britons were "underpaid, undersexed and under Eisenhower."

Given these circumstances, it is natural that British memories of World War II should stress those aspects in which Britain fought alone, rather than when Britain functioned as a junior partner in the Anglo-American alliance. These aspects include Dunkirk, the Battle of Britain, the North African campaign before the Americans invaded that theater, and the campaign in Burma. The role of British women in the war effort is also significant. What follows is a brief account of these particular topics, rather than an overview of the whole war.

In 1940 the British army on the continent of Europe was rescued by vast and varied flotilla of ships hastily thrown together and sent to the port of Dunkirk in France. When France was overwhelmed, the British army had retreated to this port. Their prospects were bleak until all of those ships, great and small, arrived from England to take them home. Although they sailed home defeated and without their heavy equipment, Dunkirk was nevertheless seen as a great and heroic event. British soldiers had faced adversity and overwhelming forces with stoic heroism, and they were rescued by their fellow countrymen who risked their own lives at sea to save them. The heroic retreat has always been a favorite motif of British patriotism, thus Dunkirk was admirable.

Britain stood alone against the ferocious, undefeated might of Nazi Germany during the summer of 1940. At this time France was defeated and Russia continued to collaborate with Germany. All of the other states of Europe were either conquered, frightened neutrals, or German allies. The United States was not to enter the war until the end of 1941, so Britain and her far-flung dominions were the only forces in the entire world fighting against Nazi tyranny.

The Battle of Britain was unique in that it was fought almost entirely in the air. The German *Luftwaffe*, or air force, had the task of destroying the RAF, the Royal Air Force, in preparation for an invasion under the planning name "Operation Sea Lion." In order to carry out this risky invasion, the Germans needed dominance in the air, which would compensate for their naval inferiority. Eliminating the RAF was therefore absolutely essential as the first step of the planned invasion.

The task proved impossible for the Nazis. Armed with powerful and swift Spitfires, as well as with the reliable, slower and less glamorous Hurricanes, the RAF shot down many more German planes than they themselves lost. Except for one desperate period, replacements of men and planes came along just quickly enough to keep the RAF on top.

During the Battle of Britain, Prime Minister Winston Churchill produced some of his finest war oratory as he led his nation in steely defiance of the Nazis. He called that dangerous time in history the British people's "finest hour," and long has it been celebrated as such. Paying tribute to that small group of RAF pilots who held the Nazis at bay, he declared that never before in history was "so much owed by so many to so few."

Once they were forced to give up their plans to invade England, the Nazis sought to pound the country either into submission or a negotiated peace by launching massive bombing raids on London. The *Luftwaffe* flew over nearly every night, sending down a rain of death and destruction. But London was simply too large to demolish from the air, given the limited payloads of German bombers. Londoners themselves adjusted to the "Blitz"

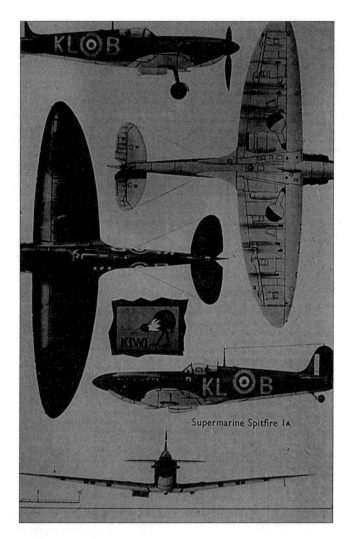

The Spitfire, Britain's spectacular fighter in the Battle of Britain.

Churchill visits a bombed area during World War II.

The East End of London heavily bombed during the "Blitz."

surprisingly well, inspiring the world with their good humor. Hundreds of thousands of them took to sleeping in the underground subway stations, where a vibrant community life soon developed.

Both the North African and Burmese campaigns received more attention in Britain than in the United States. General Montgomery was the hero in North Africa, noted for stopping General Rommel at El Alamein in 1942 during a bleak stretch when the British needed a victory. Lord Mountbatten was the supreme commander in Southeast Asia whose primary role was to protect India from the Japanese and then drive them out of Burma.

Montgomery is a controversial figure. Many claim that he was a brilliant general devoted to minimizing casualties, while others maintain that he was phlegmatic and unwilling to give battle unless he had overwhelming superiority in men and equipment. Montgomery's failed attempt to force a crossing of the Rhine in the Netherlands in 1944 is often held against him. Many critics, many of them Americans, have alleged that the materials lavished on Montgomery's campaign should have been allocated to General Patton because he might have had a chance to end the war sooner, perhaps by reaching Berlin before the Russians.

Despite such controversy, Montgomery, Patton and several other noted generals pulled together under Eisenhower to bring British and American forces to the heart of what was supposed to have been Hitler's thousand-year Reich. It was a time of great men doing great deeds for great principles.

Women did great deeds as well. Britain mobilized its citizenry to a full extent, much more so than their American allies. All able-bodied young women were drafted into national service. They had the choice of serving in uniform in several branches, working as farm laborers, or working in wartime factories. In each case they performed heroically, serving a country that was under siege for several years and subject to terror from the skies throughout the war.

THE QUIET REVOLUTION AND THE AGE OF AUSTERITY: 1945-1951

In the time between V-E Day, Victory in Europe Day in May 1945, and V-J Day, Victory over Japan Day in August 1945, Winston Churchill and his Conservative Party were tossed out by the electorate despite his soaring world reputation as a great war leader. This dramatic and unexpected defeat did not stem from any lack of gratitude for the way Churchill had resolutely prosecuted the war. Instead, it came from a realization by the majority that the Labour Party had a program for social improvement while the Conservatives' plans were extremely vague. Many recalled the depression, unemployment and economic dislocation that had greeted the veterans upon their return home after World War I. The electorate wanted a program designed to avoid such hardship.

Labour planned to inaugurate the welfare state by building up the public sector while carefully regulating the private sector of the economy. Under the calm, unassuming, and somewhat colorless prime minister, Clement Attlee, changes came so quickly that the period between 1945 and 1951 was called the "Quiet Revolution." Numerous industries were nationalized, including railroads, gas, electricity, airways, docking facilities, mines, and the iron and steel industries. Extensive social services for health, housing and the less fortunate were either set up or expanded.

Everyone was assured of having the basic necessities of life, namely food, housing, clothing, health care and education. The poor would no longer be haunted by the specter of financial catastrophe from illness, old age or unemployment.

All of this required an enormous investment. The British economy was exhausted from its wartime sacrifices; nevertheless, a period of continued "austerity," or hard times of scarcity, was imposed upon the patriotic, generally cooperative population until the new economy could be shaped. This monumental effort of self-sacrifice was substantially aided by the generous Marshall Plan grants of the United States, a gesture that has not been forgotten by many Britons.

This shift to the welfare state was permanent. Britain still enjoys the National Health Service and most of the "cradle to the grave" benefits that the Labour Party established in the immediate postwar years. Almost three generations of British people have grown up knowing no other system than this mixed economy of socialism and capitalism.

THE END OF THE EMPIRE AND THE BIRTH OF THE COMMONWEALTH

New Zealand, Australia and Canada, where transplanted Britons comprised a dominant ethnic stock, had attained sovereignty and self-government long before World War II. The white minority of South Africa was also self-governing. After World War II the rest of the British Empire came apart as almost all of the so-called black, brown and yellow colonies asserted their independence from the mother country. The largest piece of the Empire to go was India, which became independent in 1947—

an event involving much bloodshed between Moslems and Hindus before the new states of India and Pakistan were carved out of what had been British India.

Some violence accompanied the coming of independence elsewhere. Kenya, in East Africa, had the Mau-Mau uprising. Malaya was the scene of a vigorous British counter-insurgency effort. Britain also joined France and Israel in 1956 in an effort to regain control of the Suez Canal which had been nationalized by Egypt. The Soviet Union was hostile, and uninformed America did not cooperate in the Suez crisis. Thus, without United States backing, this attempt to renew British influence in the Middle East collapsed. This was a stunning blow to old British imperialists.

Despite these examples of conflict, the dismantling of the largest empire that the world had ever seen generally involved a peaceful transition to independence. Most English people had the good sense to realize that the days of a colonial empire were over, and that it was time to surrender power before it would be seized from them by their former subjects. So, they sought an orderly retreat from empire. By contrast, the French in Indochina and Algeria did not come to this realization, and ultimately disasters resulted.

Several British governments put this principle into practice with considerable style and grace. Splendid flag-lowering ceremonies, handshakes, good wishes and sentimental band concerts marked the British surrender of their empire. In most places, it was a good show, and well carried off. The most recent example was the handing over of the old Crown Colony of Hong Kong to China.

Rhodesia was a difficult case, however. White Rhodesians resisted majority rule by fighting a civil war against groups of black Rhodesians and by formally breaking ties with Britain. Finally, pressure from Britain and other countries led the white Rhodesians to accept majority rule in the new nation of Zimbabwe. South Africa, just below Zimbabwe, opted out of formal connections with the British long before decolonization.

Another problem centered on what to do about immigration to the U.K. from British passport holders in the Commonwealth. In the postwar years a tide of immigrants came in from India, Pakistan and the West Indies. This helped to diversify the British population, but it alarmed many on what was already a very crowded island of over 50 million people. Others were hostile to the new minorities on the basis of racial and cultural prejudices. The Commonwealth Immigrants Act of 1967 stemmed the flow of immigrants by insisting that newcomers have a work permit before they settle in Britain.

Like parents of adolescents sent off into the world, the British hoped to maintain subtle ties with their offspring. The Commonwealth of Nations has been described as "a body created to ameliorate the loss of an empire." It is a vague, amorphous body—a shadow of an international body in some respects—but it does promote discussions, international understanding, and educational ties. It has its place in a world in need of more contacts between affluent nations and poor nations.

There is much more than the Commonwealth to stand for the British heritage in that vast portion of the globe once included in the empire. Wherever English is spoken, British ideas of justice, public honesty, government by law and due process survive. While critics of imperialism may rightly point out examples of historic exploitation, racism and disregard for native ways of life, British people still have good reason for looking back upon their empire with pride. Compared with the great imperial peoples in history, from the Mongols and Romans to the Germans and Russians, overall the British ruled their subjects mildly and decently. Most Irish people, however, will strongly disagree with this viewpoint.

SWINGING BRITAIN: POSTWAR AFFLUENCE IN A NEW ELIZABETHAN AGE

The loss of this empire was cushioned by the fact that the average Briton was better off economically in the postwar years than ever before in history. In fact, economic historians, factoring everything that makes up a standard of living, estimate that an ordinary person was three times as wealthy towards the end of the century than at its beginning.

Many observers expected Europe to take decades to emerge from the ashes of World War II, but this was not the case. The Continent bounced back with an amazing vitality, populating and producing goods and services in vast quantities. Affluence came to Europe only a few years after it came to postwar America. Britain was somewhat behind West Germany, France and Italy, where wartime destruction necessitated starting from scratch with fresh plants and new techniques. Many of Britain's old industries were not competitive. Nevertheless, unprecedented affluence managed to come to Britain by the 1960s.

Imagine what the late 1960s and early 1970s would have been for America without the war in Vietnam and the civil disturbances associated with it. Britain had all of the dynamic change and growth of the period without this war abroad and

Swinging London in the late 1960s.

serious civil discord at home. The Conservative prime minister, Harold Macmillan, coined an apt phrase which stuck: "You never had it so good!" Indeed, it was true. The welfare state had raised the level of life and expectations for the poor, and a surge of economic and cultural achievement pushed the middle classes into a new lifestyle of abundance. For a while, it seemed that things would continue to get better.

Depending on their age, most Americans know something about this era in Britain; musical groups such as the Beatles and Rolling Stones were popular, as were all of those exciting and strange fashions to come out of places like Carnaby Street. Long hair, beards and moustaches, and colorful clothes appeared everywhere. Who can forget the mini-skirt? Everywhere it seemed that a new and youthful British culture was flowering. There was an exuberance, and a sense of humor, liberation, and happiness that anyone who experienced that era can never forget. In the realm of music and style at least, Britain was again the center of the world.

The 1960s became a time of permissiveness, experimentation and hedonism in Britain, as individuals gained more rights and freedoms. Gambling became legal. Homosexual relations between consenting adults became legal by Parliamentary statute. Divorce was made easy. Censorship of the theaters was abandoned, and nudity appeared on the stages of London. Capital punishment was abolished, and physical punishment by whipping was ended in trade schools and reformatories. More mental patients were released, and successful experiments with probation shortened jail sentences for criminals. All sorts of illegal drugs became available and popular, particularly among the young.

This permissive society had its limits. To treat the scourge of drug addicts, counseling and medication was provided by the government. There was also a crackdown on drunk drivers by the imposition of strict Breathalyzer testing, and on speeders by the posting of limits on motorways. Most recently, it can be argued that the health and safety of the British population has been improved by the absolute ban on private handguns and the enforcement of strict regulations to keep hunting guns safely locked up when not in use.

Politics during the sixties and seventies showed no dramatic shifts to match the excitement occurring in the cultural domain. Labour governments traded places with Conservative governments without sharp shifts in policy from either party. Various prime ministers, including Macmillan, Douglas-Home, Wilson, Heath and Callaghan, carried out relatively minor adjustments in a system that generally seemed to be working well.

The heady years of the swinging 1960s came to an end in the early 1970s, in what was a time of worldwide recession triggered by oil shortages. In Britain these years saw higher unemployment and high inflation, resulting in an economic condition aptly described as "stagflation": inflation in a stagnant economy. Rashes of strikes broke out, including those of civil servants. The government was investing less in health and educational services at the very time that a higher percentage of the population became elderly. As a result, greater strains were placed on available social services.

One major issue to arise was whether or not Britain should join the European Community (EC), which was formerly called the "European Economic Community" or the "Common Market." It became a divisive issue within both parties and within the country in general. Charles De Gaulle firmly rebuffed British applications to the organization in the 1960s. The Labour government managed to gain entry in 1972 and held a referendum on the move in 1975. Although the referendum passed, controversy about EC continues. Critics argue that an unrepresentative bureaucracy somewhere on the Continent should not be setting rules and regulations in Britain. Others cannot abide the prospect of replacing the pound with a common European currency.

Meanwhile, the Chunnel, or tunnel under the English Channel, produced yet another link with the Continent and diminished the age-old psychological comfort that British people have derived their separateness from Europe by being on an island.

THE THATCHER ERA: 1979-1990

Like many imposing figures in history, Margaret Thatcher, Britain's first female prime minister, is highly controversial, and not only in Britain. To her admirers, she was the "Iron Lady," the very reincarnation of Winston Churchill or the first Queen Elizabeth; to her detractors, she is a harsh ruler who pandered to the well off and scorned the plight of the poor.

One matter beyond controversy is her importance. Nearly everyone concedes that she was a powerful leader whose efforts were aimed at redressing the postwar pull to the left by fostering private enterprise and the market economy. She was an outspoken critic of big government, high taxes, deficit financing, public ownership of large corporations, and many specific aspects of the welfare state. She was also a patriot who was able to invoke considerable old-fashioned nationalism, particularly when she led a war against the Argentineans over their invasion of the Falkland Islands. She was always staunchly anti-communist; yet in

Mrs. Thatcher in a tank.

Gorbachev she found someone she could "do business with," as she put it.

Her style was confrontational, and she knew where to draw the line and take a stand. She stood up to unions, socialists, her critics in the House, and to members of her own party who wanted to moderate her staunch stands. These she labeled the "wets." As prime minister, she was an acerbic workaholic who would get up in the very early hours of the morning after just a few hours sleep, and breakfast on black coffee and vitamins while pouring over government documents and reports.

Margaret Thatcher's background is an interesting indication of the evolution of the Conservative Party in recent decades. She was the daughter of a solidly middle-class greengrocer from the provinces who played a minor role in local politics. She was university educated in chemistry, which was a particularly unusual field for a woman at that time. Thereafter she was drawn to the law and politics. Her background led her to appreciate the virtues of hard work, discipline, thrift, honesty and, above all, individual effort. Together, these are the classic middle class virtues, and it is significant that she would champion them from within the Conservative Party. In the past, Tory principles were more closely associated with the outlook of the upper classes.

At first, she was not a particularly successful prime minister, according to many observers. High interest rates, rising unemployment, cutbacks in social services, and continued budget deficits seemed to point to the failure of her policies. Nevertheless, she persevered, allowing unemployment to rise as she applied strict monetarist pressures to the economy.

The Falkland Islands War was a turning point in Margaret Thatcher's career as prime minister. Until then she was the most unpopular prime minister since the origin of the modern poll system. Her resolute Churchillian determination to fight and win was widely admired, and on the high tide of victory over the Argentineans, the Conservatives called for elections in 1983 and won handsomely, producing a large majority for the "Iron Lady" in the House of Commons. Thereupon the high tide of Thatcherism commenced.

The economy did turn around. It grew rapidly as unemployment stopped rising, nationalized industries were sold off, taxes were cut, and the budgets were balanced. Many Britons who lived in public housing, called "council housing," were encouraged to buy their homes from the government. When large nationalized corporations were sold off, or "privatized," their stocks were so widely sold that up to one-fifth of the Queen's subjects became stockholders.

These successes led to yet another Conservative victory in 1987. Then Britain, along with the United States and other developed countries, slid into another recession. "Stagflation" indicated that the freer market economy and strict monetarist policies fostered by the prime minister did not provide immunization from recession and hard times.

Meanwhile a large number of her fellow Conservatives decided that they had had enough of the confrontational leadership of the "Iron Lady." In particular, they were irritated by the difficulties arising from her negotiations over the impending closer union with Europe. To many, she had simply been in office too long and was therefore showing signs of a growing imperiousness that was increasingly intolerable to more and more party members. In the end, the party itself overthrew her—not the Labourites, not the electorate, and not the majority in the House of Commons. Many of her ardent supporters

The royal wedding of Prince Charles and Princess Diana.

throughout the country were furious at how this had been achieved without consulting the electorate or their representatives democratically. Nevertheless, the deed was done and Mrs. Thatcher retired to the House of Lords with a title and an undiminished desire to speak her mind.

For a time the Tories wondered who would replace her. The choice finally rested on John Major, Mrs. Thatcher's favorite candidate. His background was similar to hers, as he was a middle-class Tory of humble origins with solid business experience behind him, particularly in banking. His style, however, was quite different. Major was calm and smooth, and therefore more apt to bring about compromises and conciliation than his predecessor.

Most people did not think he would be prime minister for very long because an election was called for in 1992. Since the Conservatives had won three times in a row, it was assumed that Labour would win this time, especially because voters would go to the polls in the midst of a recession. But surprisingly, the Conservatives won again making their fourth victory in a row and the first time that any party had mustered such a string of triumphs since the early 19TH century. Once again Labour was thrown into disarray, but not for long.

LABOUR RETURNS TO POWER LED BY TONY BLAIR

The long-delayed pendulum of British two-party politics swung back Labour's way in 1997 after eighteen years of Conservative rule. It was a decisive swing because Labour won a large majority behind their intelligent, engaging young prime minister, Tony Blair. His politics were similar to those of President Clinton in that he took his party from the left to the center, recognizing that most voters wanted no extreme positions, left or right.

Labour in power has followed an agenda aimed at revitalizing public services, encouraging business enterprise, opposing further major privatization, and reforming the constitution. Even with its very limited powers, the House of Lords has been able to stall important legislation temporarily, particularly bills relating to Europe. The Labour Party plans to make it more democratic and representative by abolishing the hereditary peers and working out a fair system to fill the Lords with effective, able members. Devolution, or the shift of power from the central government to Scotland and Wales, has been endorsed by the Scots and Welsh in referendums held in 1997. A National Assembly for Wales and a Scottish Parliament will control local matters, health services, education, agriculture, the environment, sports, and the arts, among other things. The U.K. Parliament will still be in charge of some areas for the whole kingdom, namely overseas affairs, national security, overall economic and monetary policy, employment, and social security.

Debates about Europe have not ceased to engage members of both parties. The issue now is whether Britain should abandon its currency in pounds sterling and adopt the Euro, the European Union's common unit of currency. Britain will not adopt the Euro in 2002, when nearly all of the other states in the European Union will do so.

Northern Ireland has been a problem throughout the 19TH century and remains so at its end. In the spring of 1998 new hope arose as the Belfast Agreement was negotiated by all major parties. It called for closer relations between Britain and

Number 10 Downing Street: The modest home and office of British prime ministers.

the Republic of Ireland as well as power sharing in a new Northern Ireland government between the representatives of the two communities, unionist and nationalist. Implementation is problematical, of course, because armed and violent extremists remain active. England is not yet free from the threat of IRA bombs, as Prime Minister Blair carries out an active, engaged and intelligent campaign to bring peace to this chronically troubled part of the United Kingdom. According to the Belfast Agreement, Northern Ireland can join the Republic of Ireland in any sort of arrangement, federal or otherwise, if a majority of its citizens desire to do so.

The Anglo-American alliance remains firm as the millennium arrives. British participation in Operation Desert Storm against Iraq (1991) and in Kosovo (1999) have demonstrated the lasting close and effective cooperation between these two democracies.

INTO THE NEXT MILLENNIUM

There is a great paradox about Britain at the close of the 20TH century. Never before have so many people been so wealthy and so free. They are living longer and thus have the opportunity to study, enjoy and experience more of life than any previous generation. Yet the discontent of contemporary Britons, as well as Americans, seems to know no bounds. Filmmakers, novelists, poets, playwrights and painters all give testimony to the frequent manifestation of a restless, angry unhappiness. So do alarming social statistics, which indicate that violent crime and vandalism have increased dramatically, as well as the senseless mass violence of sports fans. And, as elsewhere, the country has

The Houses of Parliament.

its share of alcoholism, drug addiction, and suicide at all levels of society.

It is almost impossible to ascribe simple causes to such grim phenomena. Social conservatives blame permissiveness in child rearing; religious people blame the decline of faith; those who are philosophically inclined lament the triumph of materialism over trust in the improvement of human life through an ever-expanding realm of liberal rationalism.

Yet there are reasons for optimism. Continuity and tradition have always been strong forces in English history. There are countless millions of British people who still cherish the ideas and ideals of freedom, liberty and individuality. Otherwise Britain would not be such a gentle country and one of the most civilized places on earth.

INDEX